The Instructor's Guide to Teaching Writing

with

O'Hare and Kline

THE MODERN WRITER'S HANDBOOK

Fourth Edition

prepared by

Edward A. Kline
The University of Notre Dame

For Bob:
with best wishes
Ed Kline
1996

Allyn and Bacon

Boston · London · Toronto · Sydney · Tokyo · Singapore

Fondly dedicated to Philip and Vera Caplis

"Guidelines for Nonsexist Use of Language in NCTE Publications,"
revised edition, 1985, and "Guidelines for the Holistic Evaluation of
Writing," 1983, both reprinted by permission of the National Council of
Teachers of English, Urbana, IL.

Copyright © 1996, 1993, 1989, 1986 by Allyn & Bacon
A Simon & Schuster Company
Needham Heights, Massachusetts 02194

ISBN 0-205-19634-9

Printed in the United States of America

10 9 8 7 6 5 4 3 2 1   00 99 98 97 96

CONTENTS

PART I. PREPARING

CHAPTER 1. WHY DO WE TEACH WRITING?

Teaching writing is an enormously complex, yet rewarding, task. As Toby Fulwiler points out in an article from the <u>Chronicle of Higher Education</u>, teaching writing is one of the most important jobs in higher education. "I've always considered teaching writing to be among the very best jobs in the university--best, that is, if you value teaching small classes where your primary business is helping students learn to think imaginatively, reason critically, and express themselves clearly, and where it matters who your students are, where they come from, and what they believe" (104). In a writing class, students begin to think seriously and critically about how they see the world and their place in it. They systematically interact with an interested, thoughtful teacher who reads and responds to what they have written; students share their work with their peers in response groups to find out first-hand how their words and thoughts have affected a reader; and they rethink and rewrite in light of the feedback they have received. In many cases a beginning writing class provides one of the first experiences college students have with a teacher who works with them as individuals and values what they have to say.

You, the teacher, are an important person in your student's lives. Not only are you their coach and guide through the often difficult, even tortuous, process of putting thoughts into words and words on paper, but you often become their friend and confidant, not just a distant face behind a far-off podium, but a real person with honest responses to their writing. Committing our thoughts to print and then putting those thoughts into a public forum for scrutiny by readers can be a daunting, intimidating task. You have a tremendous challenge as a writing teacher with equally large rewards. You have the opportunity to provide your students with a relatively safe environment in which to try out their ideas: an environment that allows them to rethink and rework, along with their classmates, as they seek to express themselves clearly, perhaps even eloquently, on subjects of importance to them.

A writing class is a workshop in the best sense of the term. You might think of your writing class as analogous to a pottery or painting class. Imagine an art studio in which each student busily works at an individual project: The teacher circulates from student to student, studying, appraising, commenting on their work; the students occasionally chat among themselves, posing questions, making suggestions, sharing ideas; the teacher, noticing a particularly striking piece of work, calls it to the class's attention and they talk together for a few minutes about how the artist achieved the intended effect. The art studio illustrates the creative process of testing and revising one's vision in light of responses received from a sensitive audience, which is what the best writing classes do as well.

Why do we teach writing? Aren't good writers born, not made? (Just as good artists are born, not made?) Ask an art teacher in a class such as the one just described and she will tell you that, yes, varying degrees of talent exist among artists; however, at the same time, some elements of craftsmanship are teachable, as well as artistic skills that can be learned. Similarly, when teaching writing, we know that every student can improve his or her writing skills through guided practice with the help of a sensitive teacher-coach. Writing teachers teach their students, not just their subject.

As you think about why you are teaching writing to the students who are before you in the context of your particular college or university's writing program, you might consider your own purposes and goals more directly. Certainly your main goal is to help your students to improve, but improve how? Do you want them to improve their writing skills so they can write in English that conforms to the standard? Do you want them to be able to express their personal thoughts and thereby to grow as individuals? Perhaps your main purpose is to provide them with an introduction to academic work so they will be successful in their other college courses? Or, perhaps you are interested in teaching your students to argue persuasively, convincing their readers to adopt their points of view on particular issues? All of these sometimes competing goals may be operating in the writing classroom, and other goals may be present as well.

It might be helpful at this point to turn to writing theory to shed some light on the seemingly conflicting goals and philosophies of teaching writing. When describing the act of communication, many theorists speak of the "communications triangle," which includes a <u>writer</u> interacting with a <u>reader</u> about a particular <u>subject</u> in an effort to represent that writer's <u>message</u> or interpretation of that subject (Lindemann 12).

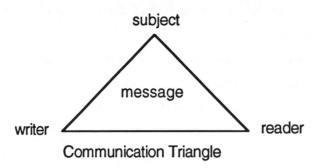

Communication Triangle

As Lindemann points out, this triangle may be helpful to students because it illustrates the rhetorical problems that a writer must solve in order to communicate with an audience: "What do I know about my subject? (writer-subject relationship); Who is my audience?

(writer-reader relationship); What does my audience need to know to understand the subject? (reader-subject relationship)" (12).

The communications triangle may also be useful to writing teachers because it helps us to understand the sometimes competing emphases in particular writing philosophies. As Fulkerson points out in his article "Four Philosophies of Composition," any point on the communications triangle can be emphasized as a goal for a writing course: Courses that emphasize the writer and the writer's personal growth are often based on the "expressive" philosophy; courses that emphasize the subject and the correspondence of the text with reality may be based on a "mimetic" philosophy; when the course emphasis is on the effect of a text on an audience, the philosophy is "rhetorical"; and, finally, when the emphasis centers on the internal traits of the work itself, the philosophy is "formalist" (343).

As you think through your own goals and philosophies for teaching writing, it may be helpful to consider the characteristics Fulkerson applies to each philosophy. The formalist theories stress "certain internal forms" with the common value that "good writing is 'correct' writing at the sentence level" (Fulkerson 344). The formalist approach, which held sway in the teaching of writing for many years, stresses the written product over the process the writer uses to arrive at that product. In her article "The Winds of Change: Thomas Kuhn and the Revolution in the Teaching of Writing," Hairston discusses what she terms a "paradigm shift" from the product to the process mode of teaching writing.

The expressionist or process theories of teaching writing include "non-directive teachers" as well as "experiential teachers" whose goal is to "maximize student self-discovery . . . valuing writing that is about personal subjects . . . in an interesting, credible, honest, and personal voice" (Fulkerson 345). The expressionists developed their theories in response to the overly formalist approaches to writing prevalent prior to the 1960s. The first expressionists included such procedures as "meditation" as a way into writing (see, e.g., Rohman and Wiecke). Other expressionists, such as James Moffett and Peter Elbow, stress the writer's individual growth in such works as Teaching the Universe of Discourse and Writing Without Teachers.

Fulkerson describes the mimetic theories as attempting to "see a clear connection between good writing and good thinking" in which "we should either teach students how to think or help them to learn enough about various topics to have something worth saying, or we should do both" (354). According to this philosophy, variously also termed the "epistemic" approach (see Kenneth Dowst's chapter in Donovan and McClelland), the emphasis is on critical thinking. This approach has often led to courses that are very academic in their focus on attempting to prepare students to succeed in the academy.

Finally, the rhetorical approach, with its emphasis on audience, stresses that "good writing is writing adapted to achieve the desired effect on the desired audience" (Fulkerson 346). The rhetorical approach also has as a cornerstone an emphasis on invention or discovery of ideas that can be used persuasively. A recent outgrowth of the rhetorical approach to teaching writing has been what many term the "social constructionist" philosophy of teaching writing. These theorists (such as Bizzell, Bullock and Trimbur, LeFevre) point out that writing is always produced in a social context that places constraints on the writer's intentions at the same time as it presupposes a reader's interpretation. James Reither, for example, tells us that "writing is not merely a process that occurs within contexts. That is, writing and what writers do during writing cannot be . . . separated from the. . . social situations in which writing gets done, from the conditions that enable writers to do what they do, and from the motives writers have for doing what they do" (621).

Each of the four philosophies described here may result in slightly different methods in the classroom, as the teacher seeks to implement his or her goals with pedagogy appropriate to the goals expressed. No one philosophy is correct, nor is one method better than the others. What each teacher needs to take into account when designing a course is the context at one's particular school; which approach makes sense will depend on the larger writing program goals, the student population and degree of preparation, the type of school (e.g., technical, liberal arts, professional), the course level (beginning, intermediate, or advanced), and the teacher's own personality and preferences. As Fulkerson points out, "One's value theory shapes his or her pedagogy" (344). Several authors have described and discussed the different approaches that have grown out of the various philosophical positions, including Donovan and McClelland in their book Eight Approaches to Teaching Composition. Like Fulkerson, Donovan and McClelland assert that "several 'schools' of composition . . . are thriving simultaneously, while being modified as current theory and practice dictate . . . . At present, there is no best way to teach writing . . . . Yet teachers must still develop a coherent approach that is based soundly in theory and that succeeds in practice. No approach can accomplish everything. Each is fashioned according to the specific problems it addresses and the solutions it eventually derives" (xi).

In their book, Donovan and McClelland outline eight approaches to the teaching of writing, each based on a slightly different philosophy, grounded in theory of language use or language learning, with everything from a prose models approach to a one-on-one conference approach. The authors point out as well that, far from being dismayed at the array of approaches, we should celebrate the diversity and energy they represent. "We should not be surprised to find differences, even disagreement. In the fabric of each, field and foreground are variously accented, movement of line is disparately cast, and colors are uniquely blended . . . . They simply invite us to reconsider our own teaching, our own enactment of theory and practice in the classroom. It is through such dialogue that everyone stands to gain--but most of all our students" (xv).

In a comprehensive survey of schools in the California State University system, White describes a similar array of approaches to teaching writing. The research conducted by White (and his co-researcher Polin) is reported in White's book Developing Successful College Writing Programs. He describes six approaches to writing instruction and discusses what he sees as the strengths and weaknesses of each approach: (1.) the literature approach, (2.) the peer workshop approach, (3.) the individualized writing lab approach, (4.) the text-based rhetoric approach, (5.) the basic skills approach, (6.) the service course approach (42-54). White concludes this discussion with the following sensible advice: "Although we cannot reasonably expect to conclude what is best for everyone, we can expect writing teachers to know what they are doing in the writing class, and why" (55).

As you think through your own philosophy of teaching writing, you will find that The Modern Writer's Handbook includes material supportive of many different approaches to the teaching of writing. Formalism appears in the sections devoted to the paragraph (Chapter 5), grammar (Part II), sentence form (Part III), diction and style (Part IV), and writing for business (Chapter 54). Expressionist theories inform the process of writing (Chapters 1, 2, and 3) as well as writing in the humanities and about literature (Chapter 51). Critical reading (Section 1b), critical thinking and analytic attention (Section 3a), and critical thinking and writing arguments (Chapter 6) echo mimetic theory. The concerns of rhetoric underlie audience and tone (Section 2a), writing in the social, natural, and applied sciences (Chapter 52), and writing essay examinations (Chapter 53). The research paper (Part VIII) takes its premise from a combined expressivist-formalist approach.

Works Cited

Bizzell, Patricia. "Foundationalism and Anti-Foundationalism in Composition Studies."
    PRE/TEXT 7 (1986): 37-56.

Bullock, John, and John Trimbur. The Politics of Writing Instruction, Vol. II.
    Portsmouth, NH: Heinemann, Boynton/Cook, 1990.

Donovan, Timothy R., and Ben W. McClelland. Eight Approaches to Teaching Composition. Urbana, IL: NCTE, 1980.

Elbow, Peter. Writing Without Teachers. New York: Oxford UP, 1973.

Fulkerson, Richard. "Four Philosophies of Composition." College Composition and Communication 41 (1990): 409-29.

Fulwiler, Toby. "Freshman Writing: It's the Best Course in the University to Teach." The Chronicle of Higher Education (5 February 1986): 104.

Hairston, Maxine. "The Winds of Change: Thomas Kuhn and the Revolution in the Teaching of Writing." College Composition and Communication 33 (1982): 76-88.

LeFevre, Karen Burke. Invention as a Social Act. Carbondale, IL: Southern Illinois UP, 1987.

Lindemann, Erika. A Rhetoric for Writing Teachers. 2nd ed. New York: Oxford UP, 1987.

Moffett, James. Teaching the Universe of Discourse. Boston: Houghton Mifflin, 1968.

Reither, James A. "Writing and Knowing: Toward Redefining the Writing Process." College English 6 (1985): 620-28.

Rohman, D. Gordon, and A. Wiecke. Prewriting: The Construction and Application of Models to Concept Formation in Writing. East Lansing: Michigan State UP, 1964.

White, Edward M. Developing Successful College Writing Programs. San Francisco: Jossey-Bass, 1989.

For Further Reading

To learn more about the **Rhetorical Tradition** on which much of our modern composition theories are based, see Patricia Bizzell and Bruce Herzberg, The Rhetorical Tradition: Readings from Classical Times to the Present (Boston: Bedford, 1990); and Robert J. Connors, Lisa S. Ede, and Andrea A. Lunsford, eds., Essays on Classical Rhetoric and Modern Discourse (Carbondale: Southern Illinois UP, 1984) and Sharon Crowley, Ancient Rhetorics for Contemporary Students (New York: Macmillan, 1994).

For **Bibliographic Guides** to works in composition and rhetoric, see Patricia Bizzell and Bruce Herzberg, The Bedford Bibliography for Teachers of Writing, 3rd ed. (New York: Bedford, 1991); George Hillocks, Research on Written Composition: New Directions for Teaching (Urbana: NCTE, 1986); Erika Lindemann, Longman Bibliography of Composition and Rhetoric (New York: Longman, 1987-88); Michael G. Moran and Ronald F. Lunsford, eds., Research in Composition and Rhetoric: A Bibliographic

Sourcebook (Westport, CN: Greenwood, 1984); Gary Tate, ed., <u>Teaching Composition:</u> <u>Twelve Bibliographic Essays</u> (Fort Worth: Texas Christian UP, 1987); Timothy Donovan and Ben McClelland, <u>Perspectives on Research and Scholarship in Composition</u> (New York: MLA, 1985); and Winifred Bryan Horner, ed., <u>The Present State of Scholarship in</u> <u>Historical and Contemporary Rhetoric</u>. (Columbia: U of Missouri P, 1983).

For further reading on **Contemporary Composition Theory**, some good places to begin include Stephen North, <u>The Making of Knowledge in Composition: Portrait of an</u> <u>Emerging Field</u> (Upper Montclair, NJ: Boynton/Cook, 1987); James L. Kinneavy, <u>A</u> <u>Theory of Discourse</u> (New York: Norton, 1980); Frank D'Angelo, <u>A Conceptual Theory</u> <u>of Rhetoric</u> (Cambridge: Winthrop, 1975); Ann Berthoff, <u>The Making of Meaning</u> (Upper Montclair, NJ: Boynton/Cook, 1981); Susan Miller, <u>Textual Carnivals</u> (Carbondale: Southern Illinois UP, 1991); Peter Elbow, <u>What Is English?</u> (New York: MLA, 1990); Peter Elbow, <u>Embracing Contraries: Explorations in Learning and Teaching</u> (New York: Oxford UP, 1986); and C. H. Knoblauch and Lil Brannon, <u>Rhetorical Traditions and the</u> <u>Teaching of Writing</u> (Upper Montclair, NJ: Boynton/Cook, 1984), and Timothy W. Crusius, <u>Discourse: A Critique and Synthesis of Major Theories</u> (New York: Modern Language Association, 1989).

CHAPTER 2. PREPARING FOR YOUR COURSE

As you think about preparing for your writing course, you will want to consider several areas, including course organization and administration. This chapter discusses administrative (pedagogically centered and professionally centered) concerns as well as organizational concerns (collaborative learning and student-teacher conferences).

Pedagogically Centered Concerns

Pedagogically centered administrative obligations have a direct impact on the teaching of writing in the classroom, and they include library orientation, use of computers, audio-visual aids, cultural events, class attendance, grading, conferences, office hours, tutoring, writing or learning resource center, syllabus, duplicating, and textbooks. Taking care of as many of these obligations in advance as possible should alleviate the possibilities of related problems during the course.

Library Orientation. If your library or writing program does not offer a standardized or required library orientation for students and you plan on integrating library materials into your writing course, you may wish to arrange an orientation tailored for your class in cooperation with appropriate faculty at your college library. Many of your composition students come from small secondary schools that have minimal, if any, serial holdings, noncomputerized catalogs, scant reference works, and few holdings other than popular fiction and magazines. A college or university library can be overwhelming to students from such a background. As a general rule, the larger your campus library is, the greater is the probability that an orientation session will benefit your students. However, an orientation that consists of a sight-seeing tour of the library produces questionable results. Library work needs to be integrated into your course if it is to have any impact on learning; plan your orientation accordingly.

If you are devoting one class period to library orientation, you can certainly offer suggestions to the library faculty about what you want included in the orientation that will contribute to and enhance the teaching of writing in your course. Try to plan an orientation that is not only exciting but also inviting, especially if the course will involve a research paper that will require students to spend a lot of time in the library. Although an orientation that takes place in a darkened room with slides or a videotape can be effective, it is not as informative or memorable as a walk-through orientation. Arrange for your class to assemble in the library's reference section, meet them there, and accompany them on the orientation tour, but only after you have prepared them in advance for the session. This would not be the occasion, for example, to demonstrate access to the on-line catalog. Students can practice this on their own time.

What, then, should be included in the library orientation? Avoid planning an orientation that resembles a scavenger hunt. Instead, include only whatever you, the teacher, deem appropriate for the writing assignments you plan for the course. The locations of the card catalogs or computer on-line stations, the microfilm collection, the periodical section, the government documents, the audio center, the rare books, the Oxford English Dictionary, and the periodical indexes are just a few of the appropriate places to visit, but only if you plan to make these library source materials an integral part of your writing assignments. Otherwise, the experience will be simply academic.

Even though you may not require a formal research paper in your course, you can integrate library assignments into your writing assignments. You might require that a few of the essays contain references to one or more books or journals for practice in documentation format. If you wish to be certain that your students can use the card or on-line catalog, require that they check out a book and bring it to class on a designated day. You can break the student habit of consulting only encyclopedias or the Reader's Guide for references by assigning a bibliography exercise of five entries selected from one or more of the standard reference works listed in Chapter 46 of The Modern Writer's Handbook.

Computers. What, if anything, will computers contribute to your course? Although Section 6c in this Guide contains detailed information on using computers for prewriting and drafting, you may need to make certain arrangements before your course begins. If you want your students to meet as a class in a computerized classroom or computer lab, you most likely will have to make reservations. You can help your students by providing them with a listing of the locations and hours when various campus computing facilities are available for general use as well as a schedule of mini-courses that may be offered on your campus for word-processing or other elementary computer skills.

Audio-Visual Aids. Will you be using audio-visual aids, not as a substitute for, but as an extension of your teaching? If audio-visual aids such as movies, videotapes, recordings, and overhead projections do not contribute to your teaching of writing, what justification do you have for including them in your course? If your classroom lacks the equipment for these presentations, can you arrange for your students to meet where such equipment is available on particular days? Rather than move your class, find out whether the equipment can be delivered to your classroom. Who pays the rental fees that might be required? Check these points in advance.

Cultural Events. Will you encourage or require your students to attend certain cultural events on campus: poetry readings, concerts, dramas, lectures, and so forth? What writing assignments will relate to these events? Will you need to prepare students in advance of the event? If an admission fee is charged, is it fair for you to require attendance, especially during evening hours when many students work at off-campus jobs?

Class Attendance. Some colleges have formal attendance policies; others delegate such policy to the individual course instructors. Absent students cannot recapture the class session, especially if peer collaboration or group discussion occurred. Therefore, you will want to establish a fair but rather rigid policy: Excuses for absences will be honored only under certain enumerated circumstances. Announce your attendance policy and include it in writing on your course syllabus. Then enforce it.

Grading. Evaluation and assessment of students' performances exist as requirements on practically every campus. You will want to decide what your "grading policy" consists of before the course begins. Avoid averaging the grades for all the essays written in the course; those written early will most likely have lower grades than those written later. Although all essays should "count in the grade," look for progressions in the grading that reflect a student's improvement. What grade level has the writer attained and sustained in the latter third of the course? What roles, if any, will participation in class discussion, contributions to peer collaboration, quizzes, essay examinations, and so forth play in determining the student's final grade? Announce your grading policy and include it in writing on your course syllabus. Then follow it. See Part III for a detailed discussion of assigning and assessing student writing.

Conferences. Teacher-student conferences can prove to be valuable pedagogical sessions. Although many students will seek you out for a conference on their own initiative, you may wish to require two or more conferences for all students during the course. When, in accord with your philosophy of composition, can you most advantageously schedule these conferences and where? Decide the conference dates before the course begins in case some students need to adjust their work schedules. See Chapter 2 in this Guide for a detailed discussion of student-teacher conferences and Chapter 4 for sample syllabi.

Office Hours. You will want to be available to your students for unscheduled or "walk-in" sessions. Inform your students of the location of your office and when you will be there for such meetings. Consider requiring appointments for conferences outside of "walk-in" hours. Keep your door closed at other times; otherwise, unscheduled student visits may impinge upon the time you set aside for class preparation, research, and evaluating student writing. Most teachers find that one office hour for each hour in class per week allows enough time for "open" office hours, although the number of visits per week will vary with peaks reached just after students receive their evaluated essays.

Tutoring. Does your college provide tutoring for students in danger of failing a course and, if so, is a fee charged? Is tutoring available for ESL students, physically disabled students, those with learning disabilities or reading problems? You will want to acquaint yourself and your students with such services if they are available; however, you will also want to know, in advance, exactly what writing tutors may or may not do without your knowledge as well as what kind of training and supervision they receive. Suggest that the tutor meet with you before meeting with any of your students and/or visit the person in charge of training the tutors.

Writing Lab or Learning Resource Center. Does your campus have a writing lab and/or a learning resource center that offers services to students? Acquaint yourself and your students with the nature and extent of these services and recommend or require appropriate students to obtain help there. You might consider inviting the director of the lab or center to visit your class to offer a brief presentation and explanation of the services available.

Syllabus. A syllabus benefits both student and teacher by its very nature as a course outline and, for many, constitutes a legally binding contract between the student and the instructor. Complete it before the course begins, even if you elect to use an incremental syllabus, one that proceeds with weekly or bi-weekly increments. You and your students will benefit by some sort of general plan for the course even though the specifics may not appear until you distribute the increments to the syllabus. See Chapter 4 in this Guide for a detailed discussion and examples of syllabi for writing courses based on using The Modern Writer's Handbook as well as the sample syllabus in Chapter 11 for writing-across-the-curriculum courses.

Duplicating. Investigate your department/program's duplicating policy to see what restrictions, if any, exist on monetary amounts or page number quantities and/or locations where the duplicating services exist. It will be helpful if you can provide a cost estimate for the services you plan to use during the course for your director or chair. Also remember to familiarize yourself with copyright restrictions that apply to materials duplicated for in-class use.

Textbooks. Be certain to ascertain whether your department/program has a uniform textbook adoption policy or permits each instructor to select her or his texts. In the latter case, check the book order deadline with your campus bookstore and attempt to meet it. Contact the regional representative of the publishers whose texts you have selected and request desk copies. Remember also to request copies of <u>all</u> the ancillaries that accompany the texts you have selected; make your decisions on which of these, if any, you will use after you determine how they enhance and/or extend the material in the texts.

<u>Counseling</u>. Familiarize yourself with the counseling services available on campus should you need to refer students for help. Follow the referral procedures carefully since rules of confidentiality often govern such cases.

Professionally Centered Concerns

Professionally centered administrative concerns have little or no direct bearing on the teaching of writing <u>per se</u> but are essential to the concerns of the profession and/or the college.

<u>Rosters</u>. Class rosters are important documents: They inform you and validate who belongs in your class. Call the roll of names at the first class and ask for a show of hands to help you relate a name to a person; continue this at each class meeting until you know your students by name. If a student is present whose name does not appear on your class roster, follow local practice on whether or not to dismiss the student. Save any add or drop authorizations that you receive until your registrar's office generates and affirms a final class roster.

<u>Discussion of Student Performance</u>. The written work submitted by students to you for evaluation should be treated as confidential. It is inappropriate to discuss any student's work, grades, tests scores, and so forth with your colleagues or other students by using the student's name or in such a manner that identifies the student. Such discussions among instructors in a generalized, anonymous manner can often lead to positive pedagogical effects; however, protect the identities of all students. When, on occasion, you want to share with the class one student's exemplary essay or other writing assignment, do so only after privately requesting the author's permission in writing.

<u>Confidentiality of Grades</u>. It is both inappropriate and unlawful to publicly post the grades of your students in a manner that allows anyone else to read them, even if Social Security numbers replace the use of names. When returning papers to students, do not place the grade on the front of an essay after evaluating it; place it inside the essay on the last page or the back of the penultimate page. The grade on an essay is intended for only the eyes of the author.

<u>Committee Duties</u>. If the rank of your appointment for the teaching of writing requires committee work (adjunct faculty are excused from such duty in many colleges), be willing to perform your fair share of the responsibilities, whether it

involves pedagogically related or professionally related concerns. Someone has to evaluate new texts, plan program governance, do self-evaluations of programs, and so forth, but one person need not do everything. Learn to say "no."

Instructor Absences. If you know in advance that you will be absent from class, either arrange for a colleague to teach the class or announce a written assignment, perhaps involving peer collaboration, to take place on that day. You might consider establishing a blanket policy for your classes that, if you are ever late for class, the members should begin peer collaboration on the current writing assignment until you arrive. Insofar as possible, have a colleague or the program secretary notify your class of unexpected, unavoidable instructor absences along with instructions for the next class meeting. Because teacher absences obviously interrupt syllabus sequences, such information will assist students in preparing for the next class meeting.

Collaboration in the Classroom

In the last few years, much discussion has appeared in the professional literature about collaborative learning in the writing class as a way of engaging students more fully in their own learning processes. As Kenneth Bruffee points out, success with collaborative learning has been mixed: "What emerges [from the literature] is that many teachers are unsure about how to use collaborative learning and about when and where, appropriately, it should be used" (636). However, it is very clear that the idea of collaborative learning, though certainly not providing a guaranteed recipe for pedagogical success, has changed the face of the writing classroom.

The model of a totally teacher-centered writing classroom, with students passively sitting in neatly arranged seats in rows, predates the current concern with process-oriented writing courses. Instead, one finds classrooms buzzing with dynamism: students, seated in groups of three, four, or five, talking to one another, and an instructor who moves around the room conversing with the groups in turn. At a prearranged signal, all fall silent and everyone, often including the teacher, begins to write.

This scene repeats itself daily in writing classes across the nation as instructors discover that students learn to write better by writing, that they can give close attention to their own writing as well as the writing of others, and that they actually enjoy talking about their writing. And the writing does not totally take place in the isolation of a library carrel, a dormitory bedroom, or at a dining room table. Much of the writing takes place in the classroom. Instead of no one to talk to about the writing, students freely and openly ask each other questions about their own writing, and they receive first-hand familiarity with an audience other than that of an imaginary construct or the course instructor. Such a situation strikes some instructors as odd, since, by tradition, students in the humanities have worked alone, not in groups. Collaboration strikes some as a methodology that belongs more naturally in the classrooms and laboratories of the social, natural, and applied science disciplines. Older, seasoned teachers of writing sense a loss of control in such a classroom setting and appear to be at a loss if they are not serving as the natural center of attention as a lecturer or discussion leader. But a perusal of the literature (see the bibliography at the back of this guide) reveals how useful and successful these collaborative writing and/or peer editing sessions can be.

Successful collaborative writing sessions do not just happen; rather, they require preparation both by the instructor and the individual students. An understanding of what should and should not occur contributes to the acceptance and success of such sessions. The first question you might ask concerns the proper time to engage students in collaborative writing. Anytime during the writing process (from invention through drafting, revision, editing, and proofreading) can be an appropriate time. It need not be limited to only one phase in the writing process: it can be effective in any and all phases.

How can you best organize a collaborative writing session? Collaborative or peer writing works well in groups or as individualized one-on-one conversations. Groups work best when the number involved does not exceed five. Divide your class into collaborative or "buzz" groups of three, four, or five students. Change the composition of the groups every three weeks or so after the due date for an essay passes. Freedom of movement in the classroom is essential; if the chairs are not bolted to the floor, encourage the students to move their seats into circles or arrangements where each can see the others' faces. Insofar as possible, you may wish to request that your writing class meet in a room equipped with tables and chairs. Individualized peer collaboration takes place between only two students.

How do you prepare for collaborative writing sessions? Your students will need to bring some writing they have done outside of class to the session. If they are involved in the prewriting stage, students should bring their prewriting and notes leading to a tentative preliminary thesis. Or if the work for the day centers on drafting or revision, then students should bring a rough or revised draft to class. Review the material on collaboration and peer critiques in Section 3a-b of the Handbook with your students in advance of the first one or two sessions, especially the guidelines and sample peer critiques. You might ask students to critique the first draft of the sample student essay or the revision of it in the Handbook, both of which appear in Section 3b. Some students will be reluctant to participate in these sessions at first, believing that they have little to contribute. Some encouragement, guidance, and prompts on your part will help, especially when a student realizes that participation in the collaboration is not an option.

The instructor circulates around the classroom eavesdropping on the groups, asking if anyone requires assistance, offering suggestions as well as smiles, and giving encouraging looks.

If the collaboration is individualized, two students trade writing, read it, discuss it, and write commentary on it. Some instructors ask their students to notate the reader's responses in addition to providing a paragraph of critique. After a fifteen-or twenty-minute session of group collaboration, you may then move to one-on-one conferences between the peers based on what they have read and their responses to it. If the collaboration involves buzz groups, the sessions end with the students silently incorporating the suggestions made by peers into their own writing either in or outside of the classroom setting. The buzz groups may end or resume anew as students share their revisions and/or editing with the group.

The whole-class workshop approach offers some variety to collaboration and peer editing. Take excerpts from actual student writing, made anonymous, from your current class or a previous semester, and duplicate and distribute them in advance with appropriate instructions. You may also wish to prepare overhead projections of the excerpts. Ask students to assign letter grades to each excerpt after providing some criteria for determining these evaluations. Conduct a written ballot of the grades, announce the results, and ask students to justify the grades they assigned. The ruthlessness and candor of the justifications often surpass anything a writing instructor would do!

Teacher-Student Conferences

"Conference teaching is the most effective--and the most practical--method of teaching composition" says Donald Murray (147). Advocates of the conference method of teaching often tout this method with missionary fervor to the exclusion of other methods (see, e.g., Carnicelli). Other teachers tend to attempt a balance between methods, including conferencing as but one method among many equally important teaching techniques. Murray suggests that a predictable pattern exists for teacher-student conferences, within which infinite variety is possible:

The student COMMENTS on the draft.

The teacher READS or reviews the draft.

The teacher RESPONDS to the student's comments.

The student RESPONDS to the teacher's response. (148)

Teacher-student conferences can prove to be beneficial at any time during the student's process of writing but especially so when they contribute to the student's process of revision. All students have the potential to improve their writing, and one of our tasks as instructors is to help them develop this potential. The conference serves this purpose well, especially at those colleges that lack a writing center. To ensure the success of a teacher-student conference, both parties involved will need to prepare in advance. Ask students to bring their writing and handbook to the conference and to be prepared to identify the strengths and weaknesses of their writing, to comment on their peers' and/or instructor's commentary on the writing, and to discuss the problems they have encountered during the writing process.

Some suggestions for the instructor's conference preparation include reviewing each student's previous writing in the course in order to ascertain that the student did identify the strongest and weakest elements in it, listening carefully to the student, confirming or modifying student comments about the writing, and providing advice on how a student can build and expand the agreed-upon strengths. You can also suggest alternative ways to approach the agreed-upon weaknesses, assign appropriate readings as well as handbook and/or workbook exercises, invite questions from the student, read aloud problematic portions of the writing, and share not only thoughts but also samples of writing on the assigned topic.

A successful conference cannot be a monologue or a lecture. Because the student has prepared for the conference, allow her or him to initiate the dialogue. Avoid lecturing; work at maintaining a dialogue in an atmosphere that is causal, relaxed, and as spontaneous as it can be. Consider sitting beside the student at a table to eliminate the desk barrier, which helps to alleviate the student's apprehension about a conference with the practical result of making it easier for both teacher and student to read the writing.

Any number of the points you have asked the student to consider in advance can serve as the starting point for the dialogue. Discussing strengths first not only begins the conversation on a positive note but reinforces the fact that improving writing involves extending strengths and not just correcting errors. Once a strength has been identified, try to determine, with the student's help, how it came about. What roles, for example, did prewriting, scratch outlines, rewrites, and editing play?

In your conference with the student, consider using the student's copy of the Handbook to demonstrate or reinforce some of the points you make. It will help your students to familiarize themselves with the Handbook's contents. Try working together through a few excerpts from some of the exercises in the Handbook, as appropriate, with verbal rather than written responses. If you think the student would not be at a loss, you might ask her or him to name the appropriate section in the Handbook related to the point you are discussing. This interactive work with the Handbook can only enhance its role as a valuable reference tool.

Assure your students through words and manner that you want to and can help them improve their writing. You can emphasize the universality of revision by showing your students copies of your own revised drafts of writing, which will also underscore the trial and error process of discovery and revision. Learning to develop writing skills is like learning to play the piano, paint a picture, dribble a basketball, or ride a bicycle. We can copy the techniques used by teachers of music, art, athletics: Students learn by doing. Process leads to product and the recursiveness of the process helps to perfect the product.

Listen attentively to what the student says about the writing process. Many times what the student failed to convey in writing is often rather clearly and rationally expressed in oral communication. Help the student convert these thoughts from the oral to the written form. Much about writing that the instructor conveys takes place in the classroom, but you have no guarantee that the student has understood or assimilated this information until you see the writing. You need not wait until the end of the process to do so. The conference can become an enthusiastic part of the writing process as an extension of or substitute for peer collaboration. A teacher-student conference that is a lecture by the instructor and/or that dwells entirely on the negative aspects of a student's writing is not a conference at all; rather, it is a punishment.

Works Cited

Bruffee, Kenneth. "Collaborative Learning and the 'Conversation of Mankind.'" College English 46 (1984): 635-52.

Carnicelli, Thomas. "The Writing Conference: A One-to-One Conversation." Eight Approaches to Teaching Writing. Ed. Timothy R. Donovan and Ben W. McClelland, Urbana: NCTE 1980.

Murray, Donald. A Writing Teacher Teaches Writing. 2nd ed. Boston: Houghton-Mifflin, 1985.

For Further Reading

Collaborative Learning has been widely discussed in the literature. A good overview of the issues can be found in Jeff Golub, et al., eds., Focus on Collaborative Learning: Classroom Practices in Teaching English (Urbana: NCTE, 1988); Andrea Lunsford and Lisa Ede, Singular Texts/Plural Authors: Perspectives on Collaborative Writing (Carbondale: Southern Illinois UP, 1990); or Geoffrey A. Cross, Collaboration and Conflict: A Contextual Exploration of Group Writing and Positive Emphasis (Cresskill, NJ: Hampton, 1994). For thoughts on collaboration in computer-supported composition classes, see Marion H. Fey, "Finding Voice through Computer Communication: A New Venue for Collaboration" (Journal of Advanced Composition 14 [1994] 221-38; T. D.

Koschman, "Computer Support for Collaborative Learning" (Journal of the Learning Sciences 3 [1993-94]: 1-88); and John B. Smith, Collective Intelligence in Computer-Based Collaboration (Hillsdale, NJ: Erlbaum, 1994). To read about the long and varied history of writing groups, see Anne Ruggles Gere, Writing Groups: History, Theory, and Practice (Carbondale: Southern Illinois UP, 1987). See also the Bibliography in this Guide for additional readings.

To get some additional ideas about **Conference Teaching**, a good place to start is with Donald Murray, A Writer Teaches Writing, 2nd ed. (Boston: Houghton-Mifflin, 1985), which includes the useful chapter "Conference Teaching: The Individual Response." One of the eight approaches discussed in the Donovan and McClelland collection, Eight Approaches to Teaching Composition (Urbana: NCTE, 1980), written by Thomas Carnicelli, is titled "The Writing Conference: A One-to-One Conversation." Carnicelli discusses the rationale and the practical application of the conference-teaching method.

CHAPTER 3. THE FIRST DAY OF CLASS

The main activity in a composition course is writing; all else, important as it may be, must be subservient to the composing process. Despite all the administrative details that writing teachers have customarily relegated to the opening class session, writing should occur in a composition class at the opening session. Sift through the administrative concerns for your course (see Chapter 2 in this Guide) and determine which of these can be delayed until after the first class meeting.

Why write during the opening class? It will introduce your students to the fact that writing will be a part of practically every class meeting. It will introduce them to prewriting, and it will serve as the starting point for your students' diagnostic essays that you will request them to submit at the second class meeting.

One of your goals the first day of class will be to establish a "comfort zone" in your classroom, wherein students feel comfortable talking about their work with each other and sharing ideas. Your first "diagnostic" writing assignment can help to establish this atmosphere at the same time as it gives you important information about your students and their abilities.

An idea that works well comes from Tchudi and Mitchell's book Explorations in the Teaching of English. They suggest that students write a letter of introduction to the teacher as an opening assignment, telling a bit about themselves as students and articulating their expectations, and their fears, about taking a writing course. We can begin this assignment by each of us, as teachers, writing our own letter of introduction to our students, letters to which the students then are asked to respond.

In order to introduce your class to the process approach to writing from the outset, allow your students to talk with each other in small groups about your letter of introduction, their reactions to it, and their ideas regarding their own responses. After they have had a chance to discuss with each other, you might have them freewrite for ten minutes to get them started on writing their own letters of introduction.

One of the advantages of the assignment just described is that it provides the students in your class a rhetorical situation in which their writing occurs; that is, they are writing to a real audience (you) for a real purpose (introduce themselves) on a subject about which they are expert (their own expectations and trepidations). James Williams calls this kind of assignment "pragmatic": "The pragmatic view of writing instruction, then, uses the process view as its foundation and builds on it by increasing the emphasis on the social aspects of writing. It advocates the position that written discourse, like oral discourse, is highly functional. The implication for instruction is that every task be related to the 'real world' " (12).

Another approach is to assign a very general topic for a diagnostic essay: love, solitude, beauty, isolation, patriotism, sports, gun control, and so forth. Explain what brainstorming is, and ask your students to do it on the topic for eight minutes. Next, explain clustering or freewriting and allot five minutes to one of these activities. Then divide your class into peer collaborative (buzz) groups of no more than four or five members each. Explain some basic concepts of peer collaboration (see Section 2c in this Guide) and allow them to "buzz" for ten minutes as they discuss narrowing their topics to arrive at a purpose statement. Circulate among the groups and eavesdrop; offer advice only if a group appears to be making no progress. Strictly enforce all time limits on this first day. Stop the collaboration at the appointed time and announce that a first draft, which you will read, will be due at the next class meeting. Resist responding to any further inquiries about the essay; return to your administrative announcements.

This procedure will strike some of your students and, indeed, colleagues, as unusual, but it serves a number of purposes. Many but not all of your students were introduced to the writing process in their secondary schools, and most of those who were usually short-circuited the process by waiting until the night before an essay was due to begin writing it. For these students, your aim will be to convince them that writing well and successfully is a process that begins many days before a product is due. And you will want to structure your subsequent essay assignments to reinforce this fact. For those students not familiar with the writing process per se, you will have provided an introduction, however briefly, to some prewriting techniques.

You will receive students' diagnostic letters of introduction or essays at the second class session; read them before the third class meeting. Make no marks or place no comments on these essays; instead, write yourself notes on a separate sheet of paper as you read each student's essay. Note his or her ability or lack thereof in the following areas: appropriate rhetorical sense of audience and purpose, composing an introduction, topic sentences, the patterns of paragraph development, transitional words or phrases, and composing a conclusion. Note the presence or absence of fragments, comma splices, run-ons, sentence variety, misplaced modifiers, and agreement (subject-verb and pronoun-antecedent). Note the skill levels in punctuation, mechanics, and format. After reading the diagnostic essays, you will have a good idea of your students' skill levels, bearing in mind, of course, that they did not have the advantages that accrue when using the writing process.

You have deliberately subverted the writing process with this assignment in order to be able to empirically validate for your students that they will write better when they do use the process. How will you do that? Make copies of the diagnostic writing, which you will again return to the students at the beginning of the last third of the course. You will then ask them to evaluate this diagnostic writing, assign it a grade, and append a commentary. This assignment usually convinces even the most reticent among your students that they have made progress in their writing during the course. Remember, as helpful as an instructor's lectures or class discussions or peer collaboration can be, students learn to write better by writing; therefore, begin writing at the first class meeting.

Most teachers want to make their writing assignments interesting, practical, and fun. Select the topic for this diagnostic writing carefully. Make it realistically challenging. Often, in writing courses, each individual student's progress, especially if slow, tends to become blurred in the teacher's mind. When you return the diagnostic writing to the students near the end of the course, it is not only they who are surprised at the improvements in their writing—so is the instructor, a moment that constitutes one of the many joys of teaching writing.

Works Cited

Tchudi, Stephen, and Diana Mitchell. Explorations in the Teaching of English. 3rd ed. New York: Harper & Row, 1989.

Williams, James D. Preparing to Teach Writing. Belmont, CA: Wadsworth, 1989.

For Further Reading

For additional practical advice on teaching your composition course, consult Thomas Newkirk, ed., Nuts and Bolts, A Practical Guide to Teaching College Composition (Portsmouth, NH: Boynton-Cook, 1993; Joseph Patraglia-Bahri, ed., Reconceiving Writing, Rethinking Writing Instruction (Hillsdale, NJ: Erlbaum, 1995); Elizabeth Randin, Seeing Yourself As a Teacher: Conversations with Five New Teachers in a University Writing Program (Urbana, IL: National Council of Teachers of English, 1994); and Rai Peterson, The Writing Teacher's Companion: Planning, Teaching, and Evaluating in the Composition Classroom (Boston: Houghton-Mifflin, 1995).

CHAPTER 4. THE SYLLABUS

Creating a syllabus for your composition class allows you to plan a rational sequence of events for the course in advance. When completed, the syllabus informs your students of the particular topics, reading assignments, exercises, writing assignments, and examinations included in the course, as well as when they will occur and what students' responsibilities are in relation to the scheduled activity for each class session. Your syllabus will most likely also impart specific information on course objectives, attendance, evaluation policies, and plagiarism to help prevent confusion among the students. It will allow those who wish to do so to plan in advance the time they will need to meet your expectations.

Preparing the Syllabus

Having obtained copies of the texts for your course, whether selected by you or a committee, begin the preparation of your syllabus by first reading the texts. As you read, look for sections and passages that you think will require elaboration in class and note them. Are the exercises sufficient in number and scope? If not, which ones will require expansion? Check the exercises in the workbook that accompanies the Handbook. Perhaps some of these exercises are appropriate for all or some of your students. Next, consider how your texts will mesh with and enhance your philosophy of composition and/or the departmental/program requirements for your course. Determine a temporary order of events to achieve subject matter coverage with no attention at this point to calendar dates. An example of minimal course coverage might include the following:

PREWRITING: brainstorming, freewriting, clustering, pentad, delimitation, temporary thesis statement, introduction, sentence combining, conclusion, drafting;

REVISION: paragraphs and topic sentences, patterns of development (narration, description, classification, comparison and contrast, analogy, definition, process, example and illustration, cause and effect), peer critiques, unity, coherence, emphasis, transitions, argument, tone, audience, optional research paper with working bibliography and documentation;

EDITING: punctuation, mechanics, format, spelling;

OTHER: writing essay examinations, writing literary analysis, writing the job application letter and the resume, orientation to the college library.

What role will peer collaboration play in your sequence of subjects? How often will you require student-teacher conferences? Where will you place the items listed as "OTHER" in your sequence?

Once you are satisfied with the range and sequence of your subject coverage, next determine how best to present each topic; for example, class discussion, lecture, peer collaboration, buzz groups, and so forth. Where can you best use audio-visual aids to extend and enhance your teaching? Will library orientation be included in your course and will it take place in the library? Where, if possible, can computers be used advantageously in your class? Will the diagnostic essay be started during the first class session and/or assigned as homework for the second class session?

Now consider the minimal formal writing requirement that must be met in the course, determined either by your department/program or you, and decide the due dates for the essays. An even distribution of due dates throughout the semester or quarter has advantages, since you are teaching a discipline that invites a skill that improves with practice. It also benefits the instructor: you can plan to stress various writing skills with each assignment through a programmed approach, and you can plan in advance the time you will need to reserve for evaluating essays. Two fifteen-page essays may not be as beneficial for the student as 6 five-page essays. If your course includes literature or another subject matter other than composition, will you require an in-class or out-of-class midterm and final or other examinations on this subject matter? If so, fit these into the sequence.

Consult the academic calendar for the entire semester or quarter and block out the days that classes do not meet. Divide the time available first into weeks, then into individual class meetings, and begin the scheduling from your sequence worksheets. Insofar as possible, try to include for each class session the topic or activity for the day, the page numbers of required readings, the pedagogical methodology the students can expect (collaboration, discussion and so on.), and what writing assignment is due that day. Provide, as a minimum, at least a week's notice when an essay will be due. The complexity of this scheduling will undoubtedly require you to adjust your preliminary syllabus plans a number of times.

Your syllabus can begin with a statement of the course objectives as described by the college bulletin, the department/program, or you. Including an attendance policy also proves valuable: one shared by the entire college, the department or program, or of your own devising. Whatever the attendance policy is, **be consistent** in enforcing it. Finally, a brief statement announcing what plagiarism is and the penalties for it may prove useful. (Consult the sample syllabi that follow for an example.)

A syllabus, of course, represents an ideal arrived at in the privacy of your office or study. Despite your years of teaching experience or lack of it, the order in which you cover the subject matter most likely will not change. But, dependent on your students' skills, the time you allot for subject matter most likely will change. Although the syllabus can be thought of as a contract between you and your students, it should not be allowed to function as a dictator. You may want to include a statement reminding your students that adjustments may have to be made to the syllabus and, when you make such adjustments, inform students in advance. Remember to duplicate sufficient copies of your syllabus to include requests from students who misplace theirs.

A course journal is a useful tool for the instructor to maintain, not only as a record of what has actually occurred in class sessions but also as a planning device in preparing syllabi for successive courses. For the course journal to serve its purpose, the instructor must faithfully record the activities at the conclusion of each class. Reviewing it periodically allows you to see how class sessions have or have not contributed to the philosophy of composition devised for the course. Meant only for the eyes of the instructor, these journals may be quite informal in nature. A sample course journal for a one-week period follows.

Week 2 Class 1: Checked on two absentees from the last class. Freewriting on "Labor Day" for ten minutes. Continued the discussion of prewriting, adding clustering and the pentad. Broke into collaboration groups and applied the pentad to the prewriting on Labor Day. Homework: consider the topic of "Labor Day" in terms of patriotism. Class 2: Called on three volunteers to share their prewriting with the class. Discussed the various applications of the pentad. Introduced the general purpose statement and discussed how it leads to the thesis. Homework: formulate two preliminary thesis statements from the prewriting done on "Labor Day and Patriotism." Class 3: Collaborative groups worked on the preliminary

thesis statements. Using an overhead projector, five
volunteers shared their thesis statements as a basis
for whole class collaboration. Homework: refine your
thesis statement and produce a scratch outline for a
possible essay of three to four pages in length.

Sample Syllabi

Sample syllabi follow for a sixteen-week (semester) course with and without a
research paper and a ten-week (quarter) course with a research paper.

Sixteen-Week (Semester) Syllabus
Course with a Research Paper

TEXTS: The Modern Writer's Handbook, 4th ed. O'Hare, Frank, and Edward A.
Kline, Allyn and Bacon. 1996. (MWH)
A Reader of Expository Essays.

ATTENDANCE POLICY:

GRADING POLICY:

COURSE OBJECTIVES:

PLAGIARISM: Using anyone's words or ideas without appropriate documentation
constitutes plagiarism. Plagiarized essays receive no credit and result in course failure
with notification sent to your advisor and Dean.

**NOTE: The instructor reserves the right to adjust the order and times indicated on
this syllabus to suit the needs of the class; however, notification of such adjustments
will be made in advance of the appropriate date.**

Week 1.   **a.** Administrative matters. Prewriting. Read "To the Student" and Chapter
1: "Preparation for Writing" in MWH; Reader, pp. 0-00.
b. Diagnostic essay due. Prewriting continued. Read Chapter 2: "The
Process of Writing: First Draft" in MWH and pp. 00-00 in Reader.
c. Peer collaboration on invention. Discussion of essays in Reader. Prepare
first draft of essay. Read Chapter 3: "The Process of Writing: Revision" in
MWH.

Week 2.   **a.** Thesis, audience, tone. Read Chapters 5a-c: "Writing Coherent
Paragraphs" and 8f: "Kinds of Sentences" in MWH; Reader, pp. 00-00.
b. Peer collaboration on first draft. Discussion of essays in Reader.
Review Chapter 5d-e in MWH; Reader, pp. 00-00.

c. Revision and editing. Read Chapters 24: "Sexist and Other Biased Language," 4: "Writing with a Computer," and 22: "Variety and Emphasis" in MWH; Reader, pp. 00-00.

Week 3.   **a.** Peer editing of essay draft. Discussion of essays in Reader. Read Chapters 47f: "Avoiding Plagiarism," and 41: "Manuscript Form" in MWH; Reader, pp. 000-000.
b. Discussion of essays in Reader. Read Chapter 9: "Sentence Fragments" and 15: "Adjectives and Adverbs" in MWH; Reader, pp. 000-000.
c. First essay (narration and description) due. Prewrite for essay two. Read Chapter 33: "Quotation Marks" in MWH and Reader, pp. 000-000.

Week 4.   **a.** Peer collaboration on essay draft. Read Chapters 11: "Verb Forms" and 12: "Subject-Verb Agreement" in MWH; Reader, pp. 000-000.
b. Discussion of essays in Reader. Read Chapters 13 and 14 on pronouns in MWH; Reader, pp. 000-000.
c. Peer editing of essay draft. Sign-up today for conference with instructor during the next week. Read Chapter 18: "Sentence Completeness" in MWH; Reader, pp. 000-000.

Week 5.   **a.** Personal conferences with the instructor this week. Second essay (comparison and contrast) due. Reflection on essay two. Prewrite for essay three. Read Chapter 53: "Writing Essay Examinations" in MWH; Reader, pp. 000-000.
b. Peer collaboration on invention. Preparation for midterm examination. Read Chapter 16a-e: "Shifts and Mixed Constructions" in MWH.
c. Peer collaboration on essay drafts. Discuss essays in Reader. Read Chapters 16f-h: "Tense" and 5d-e: "Transitions" in MWH; Reader, pp. 000-000.

Week 6.   **a.** Peer editing of essay draft. Read Chapter 45: "Selecting and Limiting a Topic" in MWH; Reader pp. 000-000.
b. Third essay (classification) due. Reflection on essay three. Read Chapter 46: "Doing Research" in MWH; Reader, pp. 000-000.
c. Discussion of the research process. Reread Chapters 45-46 in MWH.

Week 7.   **a.** Midterm examination. Read Chapters 16i, 17, and 18 on: "Mixed Constructions," "Dangling and Misplaced Modifiers," and "Sentence Completeness" in MWH and 29 : "The Comma" in MWH.
b. Peer collaboration on invention for fourth essay. Discussion of essays in Reader. Read Chapters 28, 29, 30 on internal punctuation in MWH; Reader, pp. 000-000.
c. Register research topic with instructor today. Discussion of problems in research. Read Chapter 47: "Writing the Research Paper" in MWH.

Week 8.   **a.** Peer collaboration on essay draft. Discussion of essays in Reader. Read Chapter 23: "Appropriate Word Choice" in MWH.
b. Peer editing of essay draft. Read Chapter 25: "Exact Word Choice" in MWH.
c. Fourth essay (process analysis) due. Reflection on essay four. Read Chapter 50: "Sample MLA Paper" in MWH.

Week 9.	**a.** Peer collaboration on formulating a first draft of the research paper. Read Chapters 36: "The Apostrophe" and 37: "The Hyphen" in <u>MWH</u>; <u>Reader</u>, pp. 00-000.
b. Discussion of essays in <u>Reader</u>. Read Chapter 6 a, b, d.: "Critical Thinking" and "Logical Fallacies" in <u>MWH</u>.
c. Peer collaboration on first draft of research paper. Working bibliography cards or computer printouts due today. Sign-up for conference with the instructor during the next week.

Week 10.	**a.** Discussion of critical thinking and fallacies. Read Chapters 31: "Parentheses" and 32: "Brackets" in <u>MWH</u>; <u>Reader</u>, pp. 000-000. Sign-up today for conference with instructor during the next week.
b. Peer collaboration on revision of first draft. Read Chapters 44: "Capitalization," 34: "Ellipsis Points," and 35: "Italics or Underlining" in <u>MWH</u>.
c. Discussion of problems encountered in researching topics and revisions of first draft. Read Chapters 38: "The Slash," 39: "Abbreviations," and 40: "Numbers" in <u>MWH</u>.

Week 11.	**a.** Personal conferences with the instructor this week. Peer editing of research paper drafts. Read pp. 000-000 in <u>Reader</u>.
b. Discussion of essays in the <u>Reader</u>.
c. Peer response to revised, edited research paper drafts. Read Chapter 54: "Writing for Business" in <u>MWH</u>.

Week 12.	**a.** Discussion of writing business letters and resumes. Read pp. 000-000 in <u>Reader</u>.
b. Research paper, all drafts, and bibliography cards due today. Reflection on the research paper.
c. Peer collaboration on job application letters and resumes. Read Chapter 6c: "Writing Arguments" in <u>MWH</u>.

Week 13.	**a.** Prewriting for essay five (argument). Discussion of argumentative essays in <u>Reader</u>. Reread Chapter 6a, b, d on Thinking Critically and Fallacies in <u>MWH</u>.
b. Peer editing of job application letters and resumes. Discussion of essays in <u>Reader</u>. Read pp. 000-000 in <u>Reader</u>.
c. Job application letters and resume due. Reflection on the process.

Week 14.	**a.** Peer collaboration on essay draft. Read pp. 000-000 in <u>Reader</u>.
b. Discussion of essays in <u>Reader</u>.
c. Peer editing of essay draft. Read pp. 000-000 in <u>Reader</u>.

Week 15.	**a.** Preparation for final examination. Reread Chapter 53: "Writing Essay Examinations." in <u>MWH</u>.
b. Essay five (argument) due. Reflection on essay five. Read pp. 000-000 in <u>Reader</u>.
c. Preparation for final examination. Discussion of essays in <u>Reader</u>.

Week 16.	Final examination as scheduled.

Sixteen-Week (Semester) Syllabus
Course without a Research Paper

TEXTS: <u>The Modern Writer's Handbook</u>, 4th ed. O'Hare, Frank, and Edward A. Kline, Allyn and Bacon. 1996. (<u>MWH</u>)
A Reader of Expository Essays.

ATTENDANCE POLICY:

GRADING POLICY:

COURSE OBJECTIVES:

PLAGIARISM: Using anyone's words or ideas without appropriate documentation constitutes plagiarism. Plagiarized essays receive no credit and result in <u>course</u> failure with notification sent to your advisor and Dean.

NOTE: The instructor reserves the right to adjust the order and times indicated on this syllabus to suit the needs of the class; however, notification of such adjustments will be made in advance of the appropriate date.

Week 1. **a.** Administrative matters. Prewriting. Read "To the Student" and Chapter 1: "Preparation for Writing" in <u>MWH</u>; <u>Reader</u>, pp. 0-00.
b. Diagnostic essay due. Prewriting continued. Read Chapter 2: "The Process of Writing: First Draft" in <u>MWH</u>; read pp. 00-00 in <u>Reader</u>.
c. Peer collaboration on invention. Discussion of essays in <u>Reader</u>. Begin preparation of first draft of essay. Read Chapter 3: "The Process of Writing: Revision" in <u>MWH</u>.

Week 2. **a.** Thesis, audience, tone. Read Chapters 5a-c: "Writing Coherent Paragraphs" and 8f: "Kinds of Sentences" in MWH; <u>Reader</u>, pp. 00-00.
b. Peer collaboration on first draft. Discussion of essays in <u>Reader</u>. Review materials in <u>MWH</u>; <u>Reader</u>, pp. 00-00.
c. Revision and editing. Read Chapters 24: "Sexist and Other Biased Language," 4: "Writing with a Computer," and 22: "Variety and Emphasis" in <u>MWH</u>; <u>Reader</u>, pp. 00-00.

Week 3. **a.** Peer editing of essay draft. Discussion of essays in <u>Reader.</u> Read Chapters 47f: "Avoiding Plagiarism" and 41: "Manuscript Form" in <u>MWH</u>; <u>Reader</u>, pp. 000-000.
b. Discussion of essays in <u>Reader</u>. Read Chapters 8f: "Kinds of Sentences," 9: "Sentence Fragments," and 15: "Adjectives and Adverbs" in <u>MWH</u>; <u>Reader</u>, pp. 000-000.
c. First essay (narration and description) due. Reflection on first essay. Prewrite for essay two. Read Chapter 33: "Quotation Marks" in <u>MWH</u> and <u>Reader</u>, pp. 000-000.

Week 4. **a.** Peer collaboration on invention for second essay. Discussion of essays in <u>Reader</u>. Read Chapters 11: "Verb Forms" and 12: "Subject-Verb Agreement" in <u>MWH</u>; <u>Reader</u>, pp. 000-000.
b. Peer collaboration on essay draft. Discussion of essays in <u>Reader</u>. Read Chapters 13 and 14 on pronouns in <u>MWH</u>; <u>Reader</u>, pp. 000-000.

c. Sign up today for conference with instructor during the next week. Peer editing of essay draft. Read Chapter 18: "Sentence Completeness" in MWH; Reader, pp. 000-000.

Week 5. **a.** Personal conferences with the instructor this week. Second essay (comparison and contrast) due. Reflection on essay two. Prewrite for essay three. Read Chapter 53: "Writing Essay Examinations" in MWH; Reader, pp. 000-000.
b. Peer collaboration on invention for third essay. Preparation for midterm examination. Read Chapter 16a-e: "Shifts and Mixed Constructions" in MWH.
c. Peer collaboration on essay draft. Discuss essays in Reader. Read Chapters 16f-h: "Tense" and 5d-e: "Transitions" in MWH; Reader, pp. 000-000.

Week 6. **a.** Peer editing of draft. Read Chapter 16i, 17, and 18 on "Mixed Constructions," "Dangling Modifiers," and "Sentence Completeness" in MWH; Reader. pp. 000-000.
b. Preparation for midterm examination. Discussion of essays in Reader. Read Chapter 27: "The Comma" in MWH.
c. Third essay (classification) due. Reflection on essay three. Discussion of essays in Reader.

Week 7. **a.** In-class midterm essay examination based on designated essays in the Reader.
b. Prewrite for essay four. Discuss essays in Reader. Read Chapters 28, 29, 30 on "The Semicolon," "The Colon," and "The Dash" in MWH; Reader, pp. 000-000.
c. Peer collaboration on invention for the fourth essay. Read Chapter 23: "Appropriate Word Choice" in MWH.

Week 8. **a.** Reflection on the midterm essay examination. Discussion of essays in Reader. Read Chapters 36: "The Apostrophe" and 37: "The Hyphen" in MWH; Reader, pp. 000-000.
b. Peer collaboration on essay draft. Read Chapter 25: "Exact Word Choice" in MWH.
c. Discussion of essays in Reader. Reread Chapter 22: "Variety and Emphasis" in MWH; Reader, pp. 000-000.

Week 9. **a.** Peer editing of essay draft. Read Chapters 42-43 on spelling in MWH; Reader, pp. 000-000.
b. Discussion of essays in Reader. Read pp. 000-000 in Reader.
c. Fourth essay (definition) due. Reflection on essay four. Read Chapter 6a, b, d: "Critical Thinking" and "Fallacies" in MWH.

Week 10. **a.** Prewrite for essay five. Discuss essays in Reader. Read Chapter 6c: "Writing Arguments" in MWH; Reader, pp. 000-000.
b. Peer collaboration on invention for fifth essay. Discussion of critical thinking. Read pp. 000-000 in Reader.
c. Discussion of arguments. Read Chapter 44: "Capitalization" in MWH.

Week 11. **a.** Discussion of argumentative essays in Reader. Read pp. 000-000 in Reader.

b. Peer collaboration on draft of argumentative essay. Read Chapters 31: "Parentheses" and 32: "Brackets" in MWH; Reader, pp. 000-000.
c. Peer editing on draft of argumentative essay. Sign up for conferences with instructor. Read Chapters 34: "Ellipsis Points" and 35: "Italics or Underlining" in MWH; Reader, pp. 000-000.

Week 12. **a.** Personal conferences with the instructor this week. Fifth essay (argument) due. Reflection on essay five. Read pp. 000-000 in Reader. Prewrite for essay six.
b. Peer collaboration on invention for sixth essay. Discussion of essays in Reader. Read Chapters 38: "The Slash," 39: "Abbreviations," and 40: "Numbers" in MWH.
c. Discussion of essays in Reader. Read Chapter 54: "Writing for Business" in MWH; Reader, pp. 000-000.

Week 13. **a.** Peer collaboration on essay draft. Discussion of job application letters. Read pp. 000-000 in Reader.
b. Peer collaboration on draft of job application letter. Discussion of essays in Reader. Read pp. 000-000 in Reader.
c. Peer editing on draft of essay six. Discussion of resume.

Week 14. **a.** Sixth essay (process and/or cause and effect) due. Reflection on essay six. Read pp. 000-000 in Reader.
b. Peer collaboration on job resume; peer editing of job application letter.
c. Peer editing of resume. Discussion of essays in Reader.

Week 15. **a.** Job application letter and resume due today. Reflection on letter and resume. Read pp. 000-000 in Reader.
b. Preparation for final examination. Reread Chapter 53 in MWH.
c. Preparation for final examination. Discussion of essays in Reader.

Week 16. Final examination as scheduled.

Ten-Week (Quarter) Syllabus
Composition Course with a Research Paper

TEXTS: The Modern Writer's Handbook, 4th ed. O'Hare, Frank, and Edward A. Kline, Allyn and Bacon. 1996. (MWH)

A Reader of Expository Essays.

ATTENDANCE POLICY:

GRADING POLICY:

COURSE OBJECTIVES:

PLAGIARISM: Using anyone's words or ideas without appropriate documentation constitutes plagiarism. Plagiarized essays receive no credit and result in course failure with notification sent to your advisor and Dean.

NOTE: The instructor reserves the right to adjust the order and times indicated on this syllabus to suit the needs of the class; however, notification of such adjustments will be made in advance of the appropriate date.

Week 1. **a.** Administrative matters. Read "To the Student" and Chapter 1: "Preparation for Writing" in <u>MWH</u>.
b. Diagnostic essay due. Read Chapter 2: "The Process of Writing: First Draft," in <u>MWH</u>; <u>Reader</u>, pp. 0-00.
c. Introduce essay one. Collaborative work on invention. Read Chapter 3: "The Process of Writing: Revision" in <u>MWH</u>. Prewrite for first essay.

Week 2. **a.** Thesis, outlining, and first draft. Read Chapters 4: "Writing with a Computer," 5a-c: "Writing Coherent Paragraphs," and 47f: "Avoiding Plagiarism" in <u>MWH</u>.
b. Peer response groups: bring first essay draft. Review Chapter 3 in <u>MWH</u>. Revise your draft.
c. Peer response groups: bring revised essay draft. Read Chapters 22: "Variety and Emphasis," 8f: "Kinds of Sentences," 9: "Sentence Fragments," 10: "Comma Splices and Fused Sentences," 20: "Coordination, Subordination, and Parallelism," and 24: "Sexist and Other Biased Language" in <u>MWH</u>. Revise your draft.

Week 3. **a.** Sign up for conference with instructor. Final peer response for first essay. Read Chapters 8: "Phrases, Clauses, and Types of Sentences" and 41: "Manuscript Form" in <u>MWH</u>; <u>Reader</u>, pp. 00-00.
b. No class. Personal conference with instructor. Bring essay draft to the conference.
c. Essay one due. Reflection on essay one. Discussion of essays in <u>Reader</u>. Read Chapter 7d-l: "The Parts of Speech" in <u>MWH</u>.

Week 4. **a.** Introduce essay two. Prewriting in class. Read Chapters 45: "Selecting and Limiting a Topic" and 46: "Doing Research" in <u>MWH</u>. Research a probable topic for a paper.
b. Outlining as a guide for readers. Peer responses on draft of essay two. In <u>Reader</u>, read essays, pp. 000-000. Review Chapters 45 and 46 in <u>MWH</u>; read Chapters 11: "Verb Forms" and 12: "Subject-Verb Agreement." Revise draft of essay two.
c. Bring invention materials on research topic for peer collaboration. Read Chapters 47: "Writing the Research Paper" and 48: "Documenting Sources-- MLA Style" in <u>MWH</u>. Class discussion of essays in <u>Reader</u>, pp. 000-000.

Week 5. **a.** Bring draft of essay two for peer collaboration. Register research topic with instructor today. Read Chapter 53: "Writing Essay Examinations" in <u>MWH</u>. Sign-up for personal conference on essay two. Topic for midterm take-home examination given.
b. No class. Personal conferences with instructor; bring essay draft. Read Chapters 13: "Pronoun Agreement and Reference," and 14: "Pronoun Case," and review Chapter 48 in <u>MWH</u>.
c. Essay two due. Reflection on essay two. MLA documentation. Read Chapters 19: "Adjectives and Adverbs" and 18: "Sentence Completeness" in <u>MWH</u>.

Week 6. **a.** Midterm essay examination due. Reflection on essay examination. Introduce essay three. Read Chapters 50: "Sample MLA Paper," 16: "Shifts and Mixed Constructions," and 16f-h: "Tense" in <u>MWH</u>.

b. Peer responses to draft of research paper. Bring working bibliography. Read Chapters 23: "Appropriate Word Choice," 25: "Exact Word Choice" in <u>MWH</u> and pages 000-000 in <u>Reader</u>.

c. Discussion of essays in <u>Reader</u>. Read Chapters 6: "Critical Thinking and Writing Arguments" and 33: "Quotation Marks" in <u>MWH</u>. Revise research draft of research paper.

Week 7.   **a.** Peer response to draft of essay three. Read essays in <u>Reader</u>, pp. 000-000. Revise draft of essay three. Sign up for conferences.

b. No class. Personal conference with the instructor. Read Chapters 27: "The Comma" and 28: "The Semicolon" in <u>MWH</u>.

c. Essay three due. Reflection on essay three. Discuss essays in <u>Reader</u>. Read Chapters 29: "The Colon," 30: "The Dash," 31: "Brackets," 34: "Ellipsis Points," and 35: "Italics or Underlining" in <u>MWH</u>.

Week 8.   **a.** Peer response to revision of research paper drafts. Introduce essay four. Prewriting. Read Chapters 36: "The Apostrophe," 37: "The Hyphen," 38: "The Slash," 39: "Abbreviations," and 40: "Numbers" in <u>MWH</u> and pp. 000-000 in <u>Reader</u>.

b. Sign-up for conferences with the instructor on research paper. Peer response to draft for essay four. Discussion of essays in <u>Reader</u>. Read Chapters 43: "Troublesome Words" and 44: "Capitalization" in <u>MWH</u>.

c. No class. Personal conferences with the instructor. Read Chapter 54: "Writing for Business" in <u>MWH</u>.

Week 9.   **a.** Final peer response to revised and edited drafts of research paper. Read pp. 000-000 in <u>Reader</u>. Draft a letter of job application and resume.

b. Peer response to revised drafts of essay four. Discussion of essays in <u>Reader</u>.

c. Research paper with all drafts and bibliography cards due. Reflection on research paper. Peer response to job application letter and resume. Read pp. 000-000 in <u>Reader</u>.

Week 10.   **a.** Job application letter and resume due. Peer editing of draft of fourth essay. Discussion of essays in <u>Reader</u>. Sign up for conferences with the instructor.

b. No class. Personal conference with the instructor.

c. Essay four due. Reflection on essay four. Discussion of essays in <u>Reader</u>. Review Chapter 53: "Writing Essay Examinations" in <u>MWH</u>.

CHAPTER 5. PLAGIARISM

In courses that demand a lot of writing, plagiarism has been and most likely will continue to be a problem. Your college, department, or program may or may not have official policies on the matter of plagiarism; nevertheless, you will most likely want to adopt an unequivocal stance that plagiarism will not be tolerated in your course.

If your college or department has an honesty code or other policies concerning plagiarism, be certain you know what these are, as well as what responsibilities accrue to you and to your students. You can do yourself and your students a favor by orally reviewing these policies with them at the beginning of the course. If no official plagiarism policies exist, you will probably want to establish some for your classes; however, be certain to share your policies with your program director or departmental chair first. Then educate your students in terms of their responsibilities in relationship to your code of honesty and place these in writing on your syllabus.

The MLA Handbook defines plagiarism as "another person's ideas or expressions in your writing without acknowledging the source" (26). Paradoxically, the APA Manual describes but does not define plagiarism and Turabian's A Manual for Writers lacks any mention of plagiarism. The MLA Handbook's definition serves as a basis for the definitions of plagiarism that appear in most of the composition texts and handbooks currently available, but some refining descriptors are beginning to appear. Trimmer writes: "Plagiarism is the use of someone else's writing without giving proper credit--or perhaps without giving any credit at all--to the writer of the original. Whether plagiarism is intentional or unintentional, it is a serious offense" (416). Levin goes a step further: "Plagiarism is the use of another's words and ideas as if they were your own. Intentional plagiarism is a dishonest act that can have severe consequences" (667). And McLeod reminds us of the legal definition of plagiarism: "'Intentionally or knowingly representing the words or ideas of another as one's own in any academic exercises' (Kibler et al. 70)" (8). What these citations reveal, then, are attempts to move from the general nature of the description of plagiarism in the MLA Handbook to one that is made more specific by including the descriptor "intentional."

Intentional plagiarism creates very few problems for teachers in terms of recognizing it. Unintentional plagiarism is also recognizable but the dividing line between intentional and unintentional dishonesty lies in the student's motives, not in the writing product being assessed. If one is to follow the legal definition of plagiarism, it appears that the intention of a suspected plagiarist must be taken into account. So be it. The penalties for plagiarism are severe, ranging from a failing grade on the assignment to a failing grade for the course. How, then, does a writing teacher who lacks either a college or departmental honesty code or an honesty committee confront a response to plagiarism that is prefaced with either "I didn't know it was wrong" or "I didn't mean to do it"?

No one of your students can claim ignorance of what does or does not constitute plagiarism if you devote time to explaining it fully at the beginning of the course. Some teachers require their students to sign and date an affidavit-type statement to certify both the teacher's explanation and the student's understanding of the explanation. However, a student's "intent" can sometimes be determined by examining whatever patterns, if any, become evident in the violation as well as the violation's extent. If a paper lacks necessary documentation or is properly documented except for one or two sources, plagiarism exists. If the documentation was "overlooked" or "forgotten" or is faulty in some mechanical aspects, plagiarism still exists but the question of "intention" arises. In some cases, carelessness might be easy to detect and accept when comparing whatever patterns, if any, of omission exist when viewing the writing product as a whole; in other cases, it is not.

Aside from educating your students on how to avoid plagiarism, the severe penalties that ensue when it is committed, and the values of being honest, you can consider adopting McLeod's paradigm of prevention "through good pedagogy and common sense":

1. Control and monitor topic selection for papers.
2. Don't allow last-minute topic changes.
3. Establish precise criteria for papers and don't accept those that deviate.
4. Assign the paper in stages (tentative bibliography, outline, drafts).
5. Require rough drafts to be turned in with the final draft and don't accept papers without the rough copies.
6. Require substantial changes between the rough and final drafts.
7. Require original copies rather than photocopies.
8. Keep papers on file if you assign similar topics year after year (adapted from Kibler et al., 28).
9. Above all, establish a classroom atmosphere where these practices are understood as part of the discipline of learning to write (numbers 5 and 6 encourage multiple drafts and real revision, for example), not as a rather paranoid attempt to catch one or two plagiarists. (9-10)

Above all else, treat each plagiarism case individually but be consistent in assigning penalties.

Works Cited

Gibaldi, Joseph. <u>MLA Handbook for Writers of Research Papers</u>. 4th ed. New York: Modern Language Association, 1995.

Kibler, William L., Elizabeth M. Neuss, Brent G. Paterson, and Gary Pavela. <u>Academic Integrity and Student Development: Legal Issues and Policy Perspectives</u>. Asheville, NC: College Administration Publications, 1988.

Levin, Gerald. <u>The Macmillan College Handbook</u>. 2nd ed. New York: Macmillan, 1991.

McLeod, Susan H. "Responding to Plagiarism: The Role of WPA." <u>Writing Program Administration</u> 15 (1992): 7-16.

<u>Publication Manual of the American Psychological Association</u>. 4th ed. Washington, DC: American Psychological Association, 1994.

Trimmer, Joseph. <u>Writing with a Purpose</u>. 10th ed. Boston: Houghton, 1992.

Turabian, Kate L. <u>A Manual for Writers of Term Papers, Theses, and Dissertations</u>. 5th ed. Chicago: U of Chicago P, 1987.

For Further Reading

Advice on helping students avoid plagiarism can be found in Frank J. D'Angelo, "The Art of Paraphrase," (<u>College Composition and Communication</u> 30 [1979]: 255-59) and Carol Sherrard, "Summary Writing: A Topological Study" (<u>Written Communication</u> 3 [1986]: 325-43). For student viewpoints on plagiarism see Barry M. Kroll, "How College Freshmen View Plagiarism" (<u>Written Communication</u> 5 [1988]: 203-21); William L. Kibler, and Pamela Vannoy Kibler, "When Students Resort to Cheating" (<u>The Chronicle of Higher Education</u>, July 14, 1993, B1-2); and Frank McCormick, "The <u>Plagario</u> and the Professor in Our Peculiar Institution" (<u>Journal of Teaching Writing</u> 8 [1989]: 133-46). On the causes of plagiarism and responding to them, see Dorothy Wells, "An Account of the Complex Causes of Unintentional Plagiarism in College Writing" (<u>Writing Program Administration</u> 15 [1993]: 59-71), Richard Murphy, "Anorexia: The Cheating Disorder" (<u>College English</u> 52 [1990]: 898-903) and Susan McLeod, "Responding to Plagiarism: The Role of the WPA" (<u>Writing Program Administration</u> 15 [1992]: 7-16).

PART II. TEACHING

CHAPTER 6. RHETORICAL CONCERNS

In the first chapter, we talked about the "communication triangle," also variously called the "rhetorical triangle," as a way of thinking through the rhetorical problems a writer needs to solve in order to communicate with an audience. A writer must determine what needs to be learned about a subject, who the audience for the writing might be, and what that audience needs to know to understand the writer's message. Through the process of invention, writers can learn more about their subjects. Students can also be encouraged to think about possible audiences for their writing as they determine their own rhetorical purposes for each piece. This chapter also includes a section on using computers for prewriting and drafting, since computers can provide a tool to help writers solve rhetorical problems.

Invention

Invention is an ancient, venerated art used to discover the subject matter of discourse. As Young, points out, "every writer confronts the task of making sense of events in the world . . . . He uses a method of invention when these processes [of discovering information] are guided deliberately by heuristic procedures, that is, explicit plans for analyzing and searching which focus attention, guide reason, stimulate memory and encourage intuition" (1). As the teaching of invention has evolved, it has taken a number of manifestations, from formal heuristic procedures (e.g., the pentad, which is discussed section 2A in the <u>Handbook</u>) to informal prewriting procedures (e.g., keeping a journal or freewriting). Many students have a difficult time with getting started; they experience the fear of the blank page. Taking time for prewriting, helping students practice a variety of invention strategies, and introducing them to several possible heuristic procedures can help them to overcome the "writer's block." By allowing time for prewriting, writers can focus their ideas and thoughts about a subject, explore new avenues of thought, think through the audience they will be addressing in their writing, consider what tone and style might be appropriate to their audience and purpose, all before actually writing a first draft.

It is important for you as a writing teacher to remember that there is no one "right" process of writing. Our goal in teaching students to prewrite is to provide them with numerous strategies among which to choose. Gebhardt notes that two differing conceptions of the composing process frequently appear in the literature: Those that emphasize the deliberate, rational features of the process (e.g., heuristic procedures) and those that emphasize the spontaneous, intuitive features of the process such as brainstorming and clustering. Neither point of view is "right." We need to allow for individual composing styles and to understand that composing is a complex activity that will differ by individual, by task, and by rhetorical context.

Compositionists have distinguished these two styles as the Mozarts and the Beethovens. The Mozart writers are systematic, orderly, organized. (You will recall that Mozart is said to have written entire symphonies in his mind before actually committing them to paper. Once he had a piece in his head, he rarely changed so much as a note; rather, the music seemed to spring full-blown from his pen.) The Beethoven writers are messy, creative, chaotic: (Beethoven's manuscripts, in contrast to Mozart's, are a nearly incomprehensible series of scrawls, scratch-outs, and rewrites). Some writers in our classes will be more like Mozart, thinking everything through very carefully in their head and then committing their thoughts to paper in nearly final draft form. Others will be more like Beethoven, pulling out their wildly tousled hair in fits of creative frenzy. The teaching suggestions found in this chapter indicate the richness of the resources available to teachers, resources that can help us to encourage our students to find the processes that work best for each of them. But, as their teachers, let us try to remember to allow for differences in personality and style when teaching composing processes.

Critical Reading

Many writing assignments use as a starting point the materials that the students have read. Some students, especially those new to college work, often fail to distinguish between reading for information and reading for understanding. Before a writer can interpret, analyze, or react to a written source, the source has to be given more than a cursory, surface-level reading. This advice applies to all readings (economics, biology, technical manuals, philosophy, music theory, and so forth), and not just to literature as many students believe.

One approach to invention, then, is to stress the need, value, and importance of critical reading (see Section 1b in the Handbook). The concept of individual book ownership may be an unusual one to new college students. Although they most likely have been reprimanded in the past if they marked a text, encourage them to mark the texts they now own. Show them one of your marked-up texts, and explain the system you use for the markings. You might suggest that question marks be placed in the margin where something is not clear on first reading or short, reactive commentary placed there such as "why?", "logical?", "I disagree", and so forth. Suggest that underlining and/or highlighting be done with restraint: recommend underlining or highlighting no more than one word in a sentence. If one highlights everything in a sentence or paragraph, nothing is backgrounded. Suggest, instead, placing an asterisk in the margin to denote important points as well as numerals in the margin: 1, 2, 3 to indicate tripartite divisions worthy of note, for instance.

Clearly, not all sentences or all paragraphs in a written work are of equal importance. Critical reading involves the ability to make the distinctions between which are important and which are not. Suggest that the student stop after reading each paragraph, think about its content, and underline its topic sentence. If the paragraph lacks a topic sentence, recommend the student compose one and write it in the margin. A paragraph may have to be read more than once (a concept that appears to be alien to some students) before its meaning and function become clear. After completing the reading of the entire piece of prose, the student can quickly and efficiently review it by reading only the underlined topic sentences. Then suggest that the student posit a thesis for the prose based on the underlined topic sentences and record it at the beginning of the prose. This process of analysis-synthesis can help your students become better readers.

We must not overlook the factual, informative register of reading. This level, quite important since it serves as a starting point for comprehension, can easily be tested via quizzes, but this practice is questionable as a worthy pedagogical function. Instead, devise and provide a reading guide for the material to be read that (1) includes references to specific, factual information as well as generalized and abstract references and (2) builds on the factual references and leads to comprehension, analysis, synthesis, and evaluation. (See Section 9 in this Guide on cognitive and affective domains.) An oral directive introduced by the formula "Read the next chapter for tomorrow" will most likely result in compliance but will ensure nothing about critical comprehension. In its place, a directive such as "Read the next chapter for tomorrow and be prepared to enumerate its five main points along with an evaluative judgment of the supporting criteria" helps the student to read carefully and critically. One cannot overestimate the value of such prompts.

The Modern Writer's Handbook, Fourth Edition, contains materials that can be used as a foundation to improve your students' critical reading skills. Three of the sample student essays center on a common theme, the place of women in society: "Comparable Worth in Salaries" (Chapter 50), "Career Achievement Motivation in Women" (Chapter 50), and "Contrasting Images of Susan B. Anthony" (Chapter 51). Any of the techniques mentioned previously can be applied to the critical reading of these essays, but, for the best success, remember to provide your students with some prompts. You might consider asking students to explain both the similarities and differences in the tone of each essay as it concerns women. Or you could (1) center on the appropriateness and validity of the evidence each author presents or (2) consider structure: Which of the three essays has the most effective introduction and conclusion and why?

Any of the sample paragraphs in Chapter 5 of the Handbook can serve as a basis for practice in critical reading. Many of the exercises in the Handbook contain a related content that enables them to serve a second purpose as exercises in critical reading. A listing of their subject matters follows with appropriate chapter and exercise numbers:

purchasing a car (5-1)	the AIDS virus (20-1)
propoganda (5-2)	a sculpture exhibition (26-1)
censorship of the arts (7-5)	computers in writing class (27-5)
Leonard Bernstein (8-1)	horticulture (28-1)
harassment (10-2)	an orchestra concert (30-1)
Bach and Handel (14-1)	

Observation and Journal Writing

In addition to critical reading, keen observation also serves as a starting point for the writing process, separate from or along with the use of a journal. In practice, careful observation contributes to the value of a journal. At first mention, most students will interpret a reminder to be observant as a call to keen visual perception, which is only one aspect of the activity. Being observant in this context means being alert, not limiting oneself to just the visual but also including the other senses as well.

Observation can serve as a genesis for many patterns of development in writing, especially classification and description--the types of people we meet or how one particular person impressed a student. But notice how often students will rely on the visual details to the exclusion of all other types. Remind your students that many things have texture, sound, smell, and/or taste, and that the inclusion of such details, as appropriate to the occasion and audience of the writing, enriches the writing and its appeal.

Some out-of-class activities can serve as a vehicle to provide your students with some practice in writing based on keen observation. Suggest that they crowd-watch at a particular place on campus: the library lobby, the cafeteria line, the hallways between classes, the gymnasium before a sporting event, or a theater before and after a movie begins. You might designate a thing, such as an article of clothing, as a subject for observation: socks or a necktie. Other possibilities include the textures of tree trunks on campus, the taste of water, or the sound of a car's motor starting. Some of these may appear to be difficult to do; you will be amazed at what students will write.

Keen observation can extend into the realm of the imaginative as well. "Imagine opening your garage door in the morning and finding a gorilla standing there. Describe what you remember." Or, "Imagine flying over the campus after the tether of your bungee cord breaks." Such prompts can serve as vehicles to provide both practice and encouragement for using details that are not exclusively limited to the visual. But all practice prompts should lead toward a goal of improving not only students' sensitivities but also their writing. If you do not explain to students why they are asked to write about "belts," "paper clips," or the "feel of fizzing soda," they may fail to understand and appreciate how this writing relates to the work of the course and dismiss it as busy-work. Be sure, then, to integrate these practice prompts with a purpose or a goal toward the completion of a particular assignment.

The practice of maintaining journals entered writing classes approximately fifteen years ago with varying degrees of acceptance at that time. Today few impugn the basic premise that underlies all the "practical" reasons for students to maintain a journal: it requires students to write. But, hopefully, keeping a journal also invites students to think about new things, or old things in new ways, or serves as an intellectual diary for the course, or as a springboard for the composing process.

Journals, by nature, are basically of three types: those that are private, intended primarily for the eyes of the author; those that are public, shared with an audience (instructor and/or peers); and those that are semi-private, access to which is occasionally restricted.

When deciding on the type of journal your students will maintain, determine what you expect the students to record in the journal, since this will undoubtedly contribute to, if not dictate, the nature of the journal as well as the frequency of the entries. Some suggestions for journal entries follow:

1. Do all prewriting activities such as freewriting, brainstorming, clustering, the pentad, and so forth in the journal.
2. Record your thoughts and/or impressions of any aspect of this composition course a minimum of four times a week, each time on a different day of the week.
3. Provide an evaluative description of what you contributed to each collaborative writing and/or peer editing session held in class.
4. Explain how each collaborative writing and/or peer editing session held in class did or did not help you with the writing process.
5. Record your thoughts and reactions to any of the sample paragraphs in Chapter 5 of the Handbook.
6. Record, during a two-week period, your reactions to what occurs during class sessions in both your favorite and least favorite courses this semester.
7. Use the journal as a place to explore ideas creatively.

Possible Journal Prompts

8. Imagine that the computer or typewriter you use is capable of talking to you. What would it say? How would you react?

9. Recall your least favorite memory from a composition class.

10. Classify the personality types of male or female students who wear ball caps frontwards and backwards.

11. What do you think Robert Frost may have meant in the poetic line: "Nature's first green is gold"?

12. Recall your happiest childhood memory.

13. Describe the taste of your favorite cola.

14. Explain the rhythmic appeal of your favorite rock group.

15. Record how to tie a bow in your shoe lace.

16. What does thunder sound like?

17. Recall the happiest and saddest things that occurred in your family.

18. If you were the president of the United States, and, by some magic or other, could enact any law you wanted to, what two laws would they be and why?

19. What do you like least about grocery shopping and why?

20. Compare or contrast two related aspects of your high school and college experience: homework, schedules, teachers, attitudes, and so forth.

21. Elaborate on any of the preceding items to explain how your opinion changed after you wrote about it.

Such suggestions and prompts for journal entries fall into a number of categories: personal, factual, imaginative, opinion, memory, and so forth. Directions for their use might include the following: During the first four weeks of the course, select three items from the list provided. Record the number of the item, and the date and time of your response, then spend a minimum of twenty minutes and a maximum of thirty minutes writing the response.

Journal entries may be structured (sentences and paragraphs), unstructured (of the nature of prewriting and drafts), imaginative (poetry or fiction), or any combination thereof. (Some instructors will choose to specify only one of these options.) You will want to announce how often the journals will be collected. If they are private in nature, like a diary, do you, the instructor, really intend to read them? If so, be certain to inform your students. You may, in such cases, allow students to staple some pages together to deny reading access to very personal materials. As you read the journals, write a few comments of a nonthreatening nature, such as "keen observation," "nice details," "I agree," "did it change?", "were you pleased?". What you want to be assured of is that the entries are in the journal; students, in turn, want to know that the instructor has read them. Particularly insightful entries might be shared with the class, but only with the permission of the authors in advance.

Plan the prompts and/or the instructions you provide for journal entries in such a way that the journal can serve as a device for students to use in the prewriting stage. For example, if students bring journals to each class session, you may allot five minutes for freewriting on topic X for three successive class meetings before you formally assign an essay based on that topic.

The instructor will need to designate the format expected for the journals. A separate three-ring binder works well, as does a folder that contains two pockets when opened. Consider the logistics of collecting the journals and carrying them to your office when making this decision. Specify whether or not each day's entry should begin on a new sheet of paper, as well as the amount of time you expect students to devote to recording the entries. As is the case with all written work submitted by students, attempt to read and return the journals by the next class meeting.

Prewriting and Drafting

Critical reading, observation, and journal keeping individually and/or collectively may serve as the preparation for writing. Invention culminates, at least temporarily, with the completion of a first draft. Because of the recursiveness of the writing process, invention may recur after the completion of a first draft.

The word prewriting will probably require explanation for your students. What, exactly, is it "pre-" to, since in itself, it usually involves writing? Prewriting (which may involve thinking about a topic, discussing the topic with others, and reading about and researching the topic) consists of all the writing one does prior to and leading to the composition of a first draft. It also includes any writing that the author elects to omit from a first draft. Prewriting, most often, is unstructured in the sense that it may or may not consist of sentences that begin with capital letters and contain end punctuation marks. In fact, it usually does not consist of sentences at all. It may or may not appear linearly and double-spaced on a page; it might even be arranged at angles or in circles. Grammar, mechanics, usage, and format are of no concern at this stage in the writing process. A writer realizes the purpose of prewriting when discovering what he or she does or does not know about a particular subject or topic by writing those thoughts, feelings, emotions, reactions, and facts about the topic on paper or a computer disk. Since this purpose must receive precedence in prewriting, other concerns, such as accurate grammar, usage, and spelling, are properly delayed until later in the process. Suggest that your students not even waste time erasing or crossing out items while prewriting.

Allow time during class for practice with each of the prewriting techniques explained in Section 2 of the <u>Handbook</u>. Explain the concept of freewriting; then, after setting a time limit of eight minutes or so, ask students to freewrite on a general topic. While the students freewrite, you may also choose to freewrite on the same topic or to circulate around the classroom offering suggestions to students in need of assistance. Upon completion of the exercise, ask for volunteers to share their freewriting with the class by reading it aloud. If you also wrote, occasionally read aloud your freewriting.

A variation of this procedure involves requesting each student to recite one aspect about the topic from the freewriting as you record these aspects on an overhead transparency or the chalkboard. Using colored pens or chalk, encircle related aspects of the topic to indicate categories. Then let one of these related categories serve as the basis for another eight-minute session of freewriting. This exercise results in a technique of delimitation similar to clustering, especially if you repeat the procedure for the same topic three or four times.

Try dividing your class into "buzz" groups of four to five members each, encouraging the students to brainstorm orally on a topic selected from those located in the <u>Handbook</u>, Exercise 2-1. Students may write cryptic notes to themselves during this activity. You will know if the brainstorming activity is succeeding by the noise level of the groups. After practice with group brainstorming, provide an opportunity in class for students to brainstorm individually within a specified time limit.

Practice with the clustering technique can be accomplished as a whole-class activity using an overhead transparency or a chalkboard as a collaborative group activity or as an individual exercise. Clustering can thus provide an opportunity for students to practice all three approaches. When doing individualized clustering in class, have students share their results with their collaborative group members.

Discuss with your students the seven suggestions in Section 2 of the <u>Handbook</u> for other ways to find a topic, and consider practicing one or more of them in class. Be sure to provide your students with an opportunity to practice the pentad in class: as whole-class, collaborative group, and individual activities. After your students arrive at the pentad results of a specified topic, demonstrate the various ratios (results of various combinations) possible:

action-agent	agent-agency
action-scene	agent-purpose
action-agency	scene-agency
action-purpose	scene-purpose
agent-scene	agency-purpose

47

Such ratios need not be limited to dualities; trios, quartets, and a quintet are also possible.

You will need to stress that using just one type of prewriting activity is usually not sufficient to generate all a student knows or needs to know about a topic. Suggest various combinations of freewriting, brainstorming, clustering, and the pentad. Remind students that the time limits set for the use of these prewriting activities in a classroom setting are artificial and expandable. Although a time limit of ten minutes may serve your purposes well in class for a collaborative experience with brainstorming, an individual working alone might well require more time. Suggest twenty to thirty minutes as a limit for each type of prewriting activity done outside of class with instructions for using at least two types of prewriting and requiring that the prewriting be submitted to you with the first draft. Of course, an interlude may beneficially occur between the two or more instances of prewriting.

One cannot stress enough that the writing process works best when students allow it to work. Students short circuit the process when they do not plan wisely by not allowing themselves enough time to utilize the recursive features of the process. Obviously, the process cannot work if students begin it the night before the due date of an essay. Instructors will have to act as cheerleaders for the process from the time an essay topic is announced, hopefully ten to seven days in advance, until the due date. Ask to see the prewriting after four or five days. When it becomes obvious that a student has followed the process to produce an essay, mention this in your evaluatory commentary. The effort is worth it.

Give your students practice in using the basic purpose formula in the Handbook to formulate preliminary and tentative thesis statements both in collaborative groups and individual efforts. To ensure that students are not thwarting the invention process, request that they submit the prewriting along with their thesis statements. (You might also consider requiring students to submit all prewriting and drafts with the final product on the due date.) In addition, remind students of the concerns of audience and tone. Spend time in class reviewing the checklist of questions on audience and tone that appears at the end of Section 2a in the Handbook.

Priming writing is a figurative phrase that most likely will require explanation. Literally, it means to get something into operation, such as pouring water into a pump or gasoline into a carburetor. In Chapter 2 of the Handbook, the phrase is used figuratively to stress the need that often arises to return to prewriting activities when attempts to arrive at a satisfactory thesis fail, thus highlighting one of the recursive features of the writing process. You may wish to compile a set of thesis statements that students themselves have judged unsatisfactory that could benefit by priming and share the set with your class for discussion.

Having arrived at a tentative thesis, the student is most likely ready to plan for a first draft. There are few things that cannot be improved by planning; hence, you will find it beneficial to stress the importance of an outline before writing a first draft. The outline may be of the scratch or topic variety; at this point in the process, it definitely should not be of the sentence and/or formal variety. Impress upon your students the experimental properties of scratch and topic outlines which result in the cross-outs of entries along with entry relocations, additions, and various other changes. Again, you may wish to require that students submit such outlines to you during some part of the writing process or at its conclusion along with the final product.

Using an outline as a guide, the student writes a first draft. Remind students to deactivate their editorial and proofreading habits at this stage. The purpose of drafting is to convert the thoughts, impressions, facts, emotions, and so on of the prewriting from several distinct sources into a whole, which, upon completion as a first draft, will reflect at least a modicum of organization since it stems from an outline.

Formulating both the outline and writing the first draft require a certain amount of selectivity. This selectivity may require that students disregard some materials generated during prewriting, either temporarily or permanently. Students do not like to disregard materials that they have written, but emphasize that ruthlessness and self-discipline are necessary virtues of the writing process.

In addition, while composing a first draft, some students may resist changing the informal outline when the need to do so arises. The outline should serve as a guide, not a dictator. It can be changed both while writing and upon completing the first draft. Finally, since it is better to begin the revision process with a rested and fresh mind, recommend that students interrupt the writing process after completing the first draft.

Audience

When we talk about "audience" in terms of writing, we are referring to the receiver of the writer's message, the reader of the author's text. Students need to think about this potential reader in terms of age, sex, education, background, interests, knowledge, and so on. As Douglas Park points out, "the purpose of audience analysis is obvious enough: to aid the writer or speaker in understanding a social situation" (479). But, of course, as Walter Ong reminds us in his article of the same title, "The writer's audience is always a fiction." Student writers typically need to "invent an audience in a situation where no audience naturally exists" (Park 479). The only way for students to become skillful at audience analysis is for them to practice writing to multiple and diverse audiences.

Writing is meant to be read either by its author--as in a grocery list or a diary--or, more likely, by an audience--as in an essay, a memorandum, a letter of job application, or a resume. Successful writers keep their audience in mind as they write. This concept is so important to writing that an entire philosophy of composition stresses it: the rhetorical approach (see Chapter 1 in the Guide). The types of audiences vary but fall into one of two classifications: special (individualized) or general (idealized). You will want to give your students the opportunities to write for more than one kind of audience in order to prepare them for writing successfully outside of your course.

In the secondary schools, most students wrote for only a special audience: the teacher. How often have you heard the complaints, "I can't write for him or her," and "I don't know what he or she wants." Of course, any student can write for "him or her," and if a student does not know what "he or she" wants, it might well be the fault of the instructor who has not given careful, written directions for the assignment (see Section 9 in this Guide). An instructor who does not specify the intended audience for any writing assignment is forcing the students to devise their own audience, not a bad practice occassionally, but not a good one for each essay.

In the beginning of the course, you might specify that the audience consists of the student's peers. This concept of a general audience will help relieve some of the anxiety that accompanies the writing process in a new setting and surrounding. Remind students to include the concept of audience in the collaborative and peer critiquing sessions (see the checklist in the Handbook in Section 2a). As the course progresses, consider changing the audience to you, the instructor, as an example of a specialized audience, (i.e. one who is not a peer of the writer). Other examples of a specialized audience include a prospective employer to whom a letter of job application is sent, a store manager to whom a letter of complaint is addressed, a committee considering the student author for a scholarship award, and an essay for a professor in one or more of the student's other courses. Additional examples of a general audience include the subscribers to a newspaper who read the "Letters to the Editor" column, or "John Q. Public," those people who ended their education with a high school diploma. Some collaborative writing sessions can be used to adjust one piece of writing for first a specialized audience and then a generalized one.

Knowing one's audience is one positive step; knowing how to reach that audience is another. Ask your students to enumerate the possible reactions of an audience-- indifferent, hostile, disagreeable, enthusiastic, appreciative--and then discuss how one writes to address each of these possibilities. What special needs might the audience have? What probable expectations of the audience should the writer address? Here would enter the concerns of the audience's current knowledge, prior information, biases, and probable questions as well as the length, number of details, tone, and even the organization and purpose of the writing.

Use the checklist on audience and tone in Section 2a of the Handbook as a basis for devising your own checklist tailored to each particular writing assignment. Devote some journal entries to student descriptions of various audiences. At the close of prewriting activities for an assignment, ask your students to write a paragraph describing the audience for the essay before the revision process commences. Also request that an audience analysis worksheet (devised by you or the student) accompany the submission of each essay.

Often students' questions about audience center on seeking practical advice on how much information needs to be provided. The best response is to ask students to place themselves in their readers' position. What information and how much background must be provided for this reader on this occasion about this particular subject? For example, jargon in an essay intended for a general audience or needless details in an essay intended for a specialized audience would result in audience alienation.

Any audience deserves the respect of the writer. And audiences, especially outside of academe, feel no obligation to read writing with interest and enthusiasm. Writing that sets an appropriate tone (see Section 2a in the Handbook) and contains a sense of audience reveals that the writer cares about the reader, which usually results in more than a humdrum reception by the audience.

Using the Computer for Prewriting and Drafting

Given the accessibility that most students have to computers, students who wish to use a computer during the writing process should be encouraged. Chapters 4 and 46 in the Handbook present the use of the computer for writing and researching. Writing with a word processor can also be encouraged; however, word processors will probably share the fate of typewriters within a few years because they are simply too limited in functions in comparison to the computer. Instructors can justify a requirement that writing submitted by students be typed via a typewriter, word processor, or computer. The student who lacks keyboard skills is certainly at a disadvantage today, but it is not the task of the writing instructor to teach the basic skills required to operate a keyboard.

Nor is it the task of the writing instructor to teach basic word-processing skills: formatting, saving and moving texts, selecting fonts, and so on. Find out where on your campus students can be introduced to such skills (e.g., a writing lab, a learning resource center, or a computer lab) and refer them there on their own time. But inform your students that the use of a computer does not entitle them to miss deadlines, violate format expectations, or bypass any other requirements that you set for the course.

You may have the opportunity to have your class meet on occasion in a computer-equipped classroom. Consider availing yourself of this opportunity only if you have some familiarity with computers. If you do not, find out how you can become computer literate and do so. Probably nothing discourages students more than a negative experience when first using a computer; the instructor need not contribute to it.

Assuming, then, that the instructor has some computer literacy and confidence, the class session in the computer classroom can be a whole-class, collaborative, or individualized session depending on the configurations of the machinery and the availability of appropriate software writing programs. Students, in terms of writing, can do with a computer all the things they do without a computer. But while learning to do them with a computer, some mistakes with both the software and hardware are bound to occur. Without discouraging your students, forewarn them of this reality.

As in any collaborative learning environment, the instructor will not be the center of attention in a computer-equipped classroom: the computers' monitors (screens) will be. Plan what you are going to do while students do their writing using the computer. You can secretly view students' screens on your monitor with some software programs, and you can send relevant individualized or general messages to students electronically. Or you may move about the classroom, seeking out those who need assistance. Some computer programs for collaboration also incorporate facets of electronic mail. For example, students may access each others' prewriting, outlines, drafts, revisions, and so on and then respond to questions that the author has placed there or provide appropriate helpful commentary on their own initiative. Not all computerized writing programs have these features, however.

Find out which computer programs your campus has available for writing instruction. Such programs exist for all aspects of the writing process--prewriting, outlining, drafting, revising, editing, and proofreading--as well as for various drill and practice programs for grammar, spelling, and usage. "Spell checkers" and "style checkers" must be used carefully; both have limitations (see Section 4f in the Handbook). Whatever computer programs are available on your campus, use only those that you consider appropriate for your course. It would not make sense, for instance, to recast your philosophy of composition to suit a certain computer program; instead, find a program that is compatible with and supports your philosophy.

You will need to spend time familiarizing yourself with the computer programs you have chosen for the classroom setting. As with writing, such familiarization works best if you can locate a colleague with whom to collaborate. Use the jargon appropriate to computer use when talking to your students about the computer (See the list of basic computer terminology in Section 4a of the Handbook and the format reminders for computer-generated papers in Section 41b).

If your campus has computers available for student use but lacks programs for writing instruction, begin the campaign to obtain the programs. Start with your writing program's director or chair. If neither of you are familiar with computerized writing programs, use the telephone to seek advice from your colleagues on and/or off-campus. Once you know what you want and its cost, approach the appropriate persons in your local office of campus computing and inform them of your needs. Remember, your writing students have as much a right to use the campus computing facilities as do students of mathematics, science, and engineering. Vendors of software programs, if called upon, can demonstrate these programs for you and your colleagues.

Works Cited

Gebhardt, Richard. "Initial Plans and Spontaneous Composition: Toward a Comprehensive Theory of the Writing Process." College English 44 (1982): 620-27.

Park, Douglas B. "Analyzing Audiences." College Composition and Communication 37 (1986): 478-88.

Ong, Walter, S. J. "The Writer's Audience Is Always a Fiction." PMLA 90 (1975): 9-21.

Young, Richard. "Invention: A Topographical Survey." Teaching Composition: 10 Bibliographical Essays, Ed. Gary Tate. Fort Worth: Texas Christian U Press, 1976. 1-44.

For Further Reading

Two essays are especially helpful in terms of learning more about **Rhetorical Invention:** Richard Young, "Invention: A Topographical Survey" in Gary Tate, ed., Teaching Composition: 10 Bibliographical Essays (Fort Worth: Texas Christian U Press, 1976), and Young's follow-up chapter, "Recent Developments in Rhetorical Invention," found in the second, enlarged edition of Tate's book, Teaching Composition: 12 Bibliographical Essays (Fort Worth: Texas Christian U Press, 1987). See also Susan Swartzlander et al., "The Ethics of Requiring Students to Write About Their Personal Lives," (The Chronicle of Higher Education February 17, 1993, Section 2, B1-B2). For more on journals, see Toby Fulwiler, The Journal Book (Portsmouth, NH: Boynton/Cook, 1987). (Also see Part IV in this Guide for a selected bibliography on invention and prewriting.)

To read more about the issue of **Audience** in teaching writing, you might begin with the section on audience in Tate and Corbett's anthology, The Writing Teacher's Sourcebook, 2nd ed. (New York: Oxford UP, 1988), which includes three seminal articles reprinted for this collection: Wayne Booth, "The Rhetorical Stance"; Douglas B. Park, "The Meaning of 'Audience'"; and Lisa Ede and Andrea Lunsford, "Audience Addressed/Audience Invoked: The Role of Audience in Composition Theory and Pedagogy."

For a general overview of **Computers and Writing** a good place to begin is with Colette Daiute, Writing and Computers (Reading, MA: Addison-Wesley, 1985), or Deborah Holdstein, On Composition and Computers (New York: MLA, 1987). For more theoretical discussions, see Gail E. Hawisher and Cynthia L. Selfe, eds. Evolving Perspectives on Computers and Composition Studies: Questions for the 1990s (Urbana: NCTE, 1991); Deborah Holdstein and Cynthia Selfe, eds. Computers and Writing: Theory, Research, Practice (New York: MLA, 1990); Carolyn Handa, ed. Computers and Community (Portsmouth, NH: Boynton/Cook, 1990); and Rick Monroe, Writing and Thinking with Computers: A Practical and Progressive Approach (Urbana, IL: National Council of Teachers of English, 1993). Those teachers who contemplate incorporating computers into the writing process may wish to consult the following: Michael Sundermeier and Bob Whipple, "Beginning the Computer Community: Establishing a Computerized Classroom," (The Computer-Assisted Composition Journal 8 [1994]: 41-47; Tony Deerskins, " Macintosh vs. IBM in Composition Instruction: Does a Significant Difference Exist?" (Computers and Composition 11 [1994]: 151-64); Robert S. Dornsnife, "Conversion of the Reluctant: Introducing Faculty to Computer Classrooms," (The Computer-Assisted Composition Journal 8 [1994]: 38-40); and Cynthia Selfe and Susan Hilligoss, eds., Literacy and Computers: The Complications of Teaching and Learning with Technology (New York: Modern Language Association, 1994).

CHAPTER 7. REVISION AS RE-VISION

Teachers of writing are teachers of revision; compositionists are fond of saying that "writing is rewriting." But what, then, is revision and how is it related to rewriting, to editing, to proofreading? Ronald Sudol, in his book <u>Revising: New Essays for Teachers of Writing</u>, discusses these problems of definition. He points to at least four different ways in which the term <u>revision</u> is typically used. The first is revision as editing; that is, "the use of rules, maxims, and common sense to produce an error-free text suitable for reading" (ix). But editing, although an important rewriting skill, is not the same as re-vision in the sense of re-seeing one's work. Sudol suggests that the second way we use the term <u>revision</u> refers to this "exercise of critical thinking to induce fresh discovery" (x).

It is this broader sense of revision as rethinking the text at the macro-level (making changes in structure, development, coherence, tone, style, and so on) that is intended in this <u>Guide</u>. There are yet other ways that revision can be viewed, says Sudol; for example, we can look at the teacher's role in motivating and promoting such creative thinking and, finally, we can look at revision as "the essence of intellectual growth liberate[ing] us from confinement by narrow forms of thought and feeling, from mental laxity, and from whatever is old, false, tired, and trite" (xi). In this chapter, we will explore together some of the ways in which teachers can help their writing students to revise their work thoughtfully and creatively.

Paragraphs

Paragraphs require the same composition processes as essays do although on a smaller scale. Each paragraph has a purpose--to make its topic sentence clear and developed, and a paragraph ends when it has achieved this purpose. You can help your students to revise their paragraphs by stressing the four inherent qualities that well-written paragraphs possess: completeness, unity, coherence, and order.

Completeness, Unity, Coherence, and Order

<u>Complete paragraphs</u> explain and illustrate what the topic sentence promises: no more and no less (see Section 5a in the <u>Handbook</u>). This quality relates and contributes to <u>unity</u>, wherein every sentence in the paragraph relates to the topic sentence. Any sentences that lack such a relationship constitute a digression and must be removed. Suggest to your students that they relate the content words (nouns, verbs, adjectives, adverbs) in each of the paragraph's sentences to the sentence that precedes it and/or the topic sentence as a test for completeness. If the topic sentence is a compound, complex,

or compound-complex sentence, has each clause been accorded appropriate and complete development?

Coherence is that quality which holds the paragraph together as a logical, meaningful unit: sentences flow one into another without puzzling gaps in content. The key to coherence lies in the appropriate use of transitional words and phrases (see Section 5d in the Handbook), consistency in verb voice (Sections 11b and 16c), tense (Sections 11b-1 and Section 16f-h), and parallelism (Section 20c).

Order in a paragraph results from the organizational strategy selected: general to specific, specific to general, climactic, time, or spatial order (see Section 5b in the Handbook). To be certain that all of your students understand these options, analyze in class the sample paragraphs in Section 5b of the Handbook. Ask which words and sentences indicate an order of specific to general or general to specific and so forth. Select a paragraph that displays one option of order and ask students to recast it to reflect a different option of order. Remind your students that no one order is inherently better than another order; however, of the options available, the writer selects the one best suited to presenting the material, the one that best explains what the topic sentence promises.

Ascertain that your students understand the abstract concepts of completeness, unity, coherence, and order by working on each in turn. Use any of the sample paragraphs in the Handbook, especially in Chapter 5, as material from which to extract and enumerate the specifics that constitute these qualities. Or select paragraphs for analysis from any of the complete student essays found in the Handbook (Chapters 3, 50, and 51), or from your own students' writing (but only after obtaining the students' permission in advance).

The Topic Sentence

It will become obvious to your students that the key to writing successful paragraphs lies in the topic sentence. Try to alleviate whatever fears and/or misconceptions your students may bring with them about the topic sentence. Can the topic sentence be implied? Yes, but it succeeds, as a rule, only in the hands of a skillful writer. You are probably courting pedagogical disaster if you do not require that the topic sentence be explicitly stated. Can a topic sentence be two sentences? No, a sentence (singular) cannot be sentences (plural). A dose of sentence combining should resolve this particular anxiety.

Must the topic sentence appear as the first sentence in the paragraph? Most successfully written student paragraphs do locate the topic sentence at the beginning of the paragraph leading to what is called the pyramid structure: all else in the paragraph emanates from and relates back to the topic sentence. However, many instructors favor the inverted pyramid structure wherein the topic sentence appears last, and, if well constructed, the paragraph begins on a general level and leads into the specific topic sentence. This structure requires a skill and sophistication that many of our students find difficult to master. They usually begin with a general statement that is too panoramic in scope and produce sentences that have little or no relationship to the topic sentence, which appears last in the paragraph. Can the topic sentence be placed in the middle of the paragraph? Middle positions in writing, whether in a paragraph or a sentence, do not lend themselves to emphasis. Stress that the most emphatic positions are at the beginning and at the end, which applies to both the paragraph and the sentence.

Select any of the sample paragraphs in the Handbook, especially in Chapter 5, or paragraphs from the student essays in Chapters 3, 50, and 51, and ask the students to identify the topic sentences. Note their locations in the paragraph and what they promise to the reader especially in terms of paragraph development. Then discuss how the topic sentence functions in each of the paragraphs: a partial transition from preceding material to new material, a direct statement, a definition, a proposal, a call to action, a statement of relationship (cause and effect), an illustration or example, a practical result, or combinations thereof.

Paragraph Development

Students may select to develop a paragraph by using one or more of the traditional modes of development as presented in Section 5c of the Handbook: description, definition, classification, comparison and contrast, analogy, example and illustration, process, cause and effect. Although one can effectively develop an entire essay using only one of these modes for development at the paragraph level (e.g., comparison and contrast), an equally common practice is to mix the modes within an essay so that each paragraph employs a different mode of development (e.g., definition, classification, analogy, and description). When selecting this latter option, the writer must decide, according to the nature of the thesis sentence, the most effective arrangement of the individual paragraphs within the essay.

Alternative options to paragraph development and generation include Alton Becker's patterns of topic (T), restriction (R), illustration (I), and problem to solution or question to answer. In the TRI sequence, the topic sentence serves as a proposition of relationship (comparison, contrast, process, classification), which becomes restricted by restating it in specific terms (definition, description), and illustration follows via analogy and/or example. The TRI sequence reflects the developmental order of a deductive paragraph; the reverse, the IRT sequence, reflects the inductive paragraph. The sample paragraphs in Chapter 5 of the Handbook can serve as examples for analysis of the TRI options. Additionally, the topic sentence can be formed as a question to which the remainder of the paragraph serves as an answer, many times using the TRI structure. What you will want to make clear to your students is that, regardless of the developmental option chosen, a paragraph contains movement from and between levels of generality and particularity. Paragraphs that remain strictly on one or the other level (generality or particularity) rarely succeed; good paragraphing requires the presence of both levels.

Paragraph Analysis

Analysis of paragraphs is a type of intellectual exercise that simply reveals whether the student can recognize and name the parts. It does not, of itself, ensure that a student can write a good paragraph; hence, analysis of paragraphs only works well if it is followed by synthesis and generation; i.e., the student not only writes a paragraph but can, either orally or in writing, explain and verify that it is complete, unified, coherent, and ordered, and it has a topic sentence that serves a particular function.

Another practical application for revising paragraphs is to encourage students to underline in the last draft and/or final product all topic sentences with one line and the thesis sentence with two lines. This in itself requires that the student prove that these sentences do appear. Next, remind the student to ascertain that each topic sentence relates to the thesis, usually by repeating a key word or synonym for it found in the thesis sentence. If this is not the case, recommend revision to overcome the deficiency. Then remind the student to ensure that all sentences in the paragraph relate to the topic sentence with appropriate revision as necessary. The result will be not only unity in the paragraph but also in the essay. Use the student essays in Chapters 3, 50, and 51 of the Handbook as a basis for such exercises. Such analyses work well both on a collaborative and an individual basis.

Sentences and Style

Why teach style? Students are often not motivated to explore the issue of style, suspecting that one is "born" with a certain writing style that a particular instructor either likes or dislikes. Teachers often hear students remark, "He or she just doesn't like my style." Weathers emphasizes the point that we need to make style significant for our students: "I think we should confirm for our students that style has something to do with better communication, adding as it does a certain Technicolor to otherwise black-and-white language. . . . Style, by its very nature, is the art of selection, how we choose says something about who we are" (187). First and foremost, style is choice. We can choose to use certain syntactic patterns for our sentences, and we can choose certain words to achieve a desired effect. In this section of the <u>Guide</u>, we will discuss how students can explore style at the level of both sentences and words.

Sentences contribute to and help determine both the tone and the style of writing. Knowing the audience and purpose helps us make decisions about tone and style. Many students are familiar with the treatment of the sentence from the viewpoint of grammar; most of them have less experience with the sentence as a unit of tone and style. Within the constraints of sentence grammar (agreement, word order placement, and so forth), many choices are available. These choices that writers consider and make during the revision process directly contribute to the tone and style of the writing. Be certain, then, that your students understand the concept of tone in writing (see the <u>Handbook</u>, Section 2a). Use any of the sample paragraphs in Chapter 5 of the <u>Handbook</u> or the student-authored paragraphs in Chapters 50 and 51 as a basis to discuss and exemplify how sentence choices beyond those at the grammatical level contribute to tone and style. To write correctly, we need a knowledge of sentence grammar; to write effectively, we need a knowledge of sentence rhetoric (i.e., the choices available).

Unity, Coherence, Emphasis

The abstract concepts of unity, coherence, and emphasis characterize essays and paragraphs. The same qualities characterize sentences. A sentence has <u>unity</u> because it expresses a complete thought. It has <u>coherence</u> through the agreement of the subject and predicate and word order placement. That it has <u>emphasis</u> is not as obvious as are the other two qualities. In writing we underline a word or phrase to indicate italics, which, in turn, also indicates emphasis. But a little underlining goes a long way. Skillful control of sentence structure and rhythm serves as the avenue to approach the teaching of sentence emphasis.

The writing characterized as "officialese" or gobbledygook (see the <u>Handbook</u>, Chapter 23) with its muddled and monotonous rhythms results from a lack of emphasis. In the hands of skillful writers of fiction, emphatic sentence rhythms often effectively accompany emotional heightening mainly because readers discern these rhythms. The first step in achieving rhythmic emphasis in student writing of nonfiction is to suggest that the students read their writing aloud, listening for breaks in the rhythm that lead to a boring, dull, sameness or a lack of smoothness that jars the thought process. Strings of prepositional phrases added one to another and successive sentences of short similar patterns lull the reader:

As I walked <u>in the valley by the river in the morning</u> as the mist began . . . .
<u>The rain fell</u>. <u>The car went fast</u>. <u>The street was slippery</u>. <u>The sun shone</u>.

One key to sentence emphasis is found in the finite verb. Such emphasis excludes verbals (as effective as they can be, but not, of course, as sentence predicates), and excessive use of the forms of the verb to be. Another key is found in word order. Remind your students that the occasional use of an interrogative sentence can be an emphatic device. Although word order in English is relatively fixed, some choices, governed both by grammar and semantics, do exist. We may write: "The person ate the meat" but not "The meat ate the person" even though the grammatical units are identical.

Sentence Variety

Achieving sentence variety is another function in the revision process. One way to attain sentence variety is to ask your students to underline all the modifiers used, noting both their types and their placements. You might stress that any shift from the normal expected word order calls attention to itself, providing not only variety but also emphasis. Share with your students the differences in the following pairs of sentences which result from word order changes:

    a. You are always so <u>considerate</u>.
    b. How <u>considerate</u> you always are.

    a. We have seldom seen <u>a bigger car</u>.
    b. <u>A bigger car</u> we have seldom seen.

    a. Her hair is <u>red</u>.
    b. <u>Red</u> is the color of her hair.

    a. A small, <u>tear-stained, and freckled</u> face looked up from the overturned wagon.
    b. A small face, <u>tear-stained and freckled</u>, looked up from the overturned wagon.

Adverbs and adverb phrases are movable modifiers and their various placements can provide sentence variety. Consider the placement of adverbials in the following examples. (You may wish to conduct a contest to see how many valid variants your students can compose.)

    1. The group arrived <u>here at two o'clock, as it had been instructed</u>.
    2. <u>Here</u>, the group arrived, <u>at two o'clock, as it had been instructed</u>.
    3. <u>As it had been instructed</u>, the group arrived <u>here at two o'clock</u>.
    4. <u>At two o'clock</u>, the group arrived <u>here</u>, <u>as it had been instructed</u>.
    5. The group, <u>here, at two o'clock, as it had been instructed</u>, arrived.
    6. The group, <u>at two o'clock, as it had been instructed, here</u>, arrived.

An additional forty-three variations of this sentence are possible. You might consider offering an award to the student who can write the most variations of the preceding sentence or a shorter one.

The adjective phrase modifier is also freely moveable:

Feeling tired, I went home.

I, feeling tired, went home.

I went home feeling tired.

This freedom often leads to the absurdities of the dangling modifier:

Looking to the left and the right, the house appeared.

Editing is the place in the writing process to detect and remedy such oversights. Ask your students to circle the subject in each clause and sentence so that they may then check modifiers of the subject to search out dangling modifiers.

A final point about sentence variety concerns loose and periodic sentence constructions. The loose pattern is the norm: modifiers, subject, verb, and complements appear in their usual order. The periodic pattern is one where either the subject and verb or the verb is delayed until the end of the sentence:

Despite his intelligence, industriousness, cooperativeness, and punctuality for class, Geoffrey failed.

Geoffrey, despite his intelligence, industriousness, cooperativeness, and punctuality for class, failed.

Not all sentence content lends itself to effective presentation in the periodic pattern. Careful re-visioning of each and every sentence in the process of revision will help students locate the content that is suitable for the pattern.

Sentence Kinds

Variety in the kinds of sentences written (see Chapter 8f in the Handbook) also contributes to lively writing. Most students write strings of simple sentences, albeit of varying lengths, because they are easier to compose. They resist writing the compound, complex, and compound-complex kinds of sentences because to do so requires judgments concerning coordination and subordination. Simply reminding students that variety in the kinds of sentences is desirable results in little if any concrete results. Suggest, instead, that they classify and count the sentence kinds in their draft copy. When they see how heavily they rely on the simple sentence, most students will be encouraged to make the desired revisions. Some in-class practice may be beneficial in combining simple sentences into complex ones.

Sentence-combining, which has proven its value as a composition skill in many classrooms and research studies, can be used to "give the learner control over those important internal relationships [within sentences]. Practice in sentence-combining develops skills in seeing relationships among the various elements of the sentence" (Graves 195). Consider the following example:

I drank the water. I was thirsty.

If these two ideas are conceived of as equal, they are coordinate and can be combined in four ways:

> I drank the water and I was thirsty.
>
> I was thirsty and I drank the water.
>
> I drank the water; I was thirsty.
>
> I was thirsty; I drank the water.

But note in the first and third examples that the meaning is unclear. The normal order of cause and effect has been reversed and results in ambiguity. To eliminate such ambiguity, the writer can opt for subordination:

> <u>Because I was thirsty</u>, I drank the water.
>
> I drank the water <u>because I was thirsty</u>.
>
> <u>Even though I drank the water</u>, I was thirsty.
>
> I was thirsty <u>even though I drank the water</u>.

A word or two to students about sentence length may be of value to ward off a general sameness that can dull the audience. The quantitative extremes of one word and hundreds of words in a sentence seldom occur in student writing. Successive short sentences and/or lengthy ones need not be avoided entirely but should be questioned. The limitations and requirements of our minds determine how many words we can read and comprehend in one sentence string. Unless striving after a special effect, the writer does best to regard the very short and very long sentences with suspicion. Revising to achieve sentence emphasis and variety adopts to collaborative efforts as well as to individual ones, but some guidance and plenty of reminders from the instructor will be in order.

Words and Style

Properties of Words

Words constitute the minimal units in the writing process. Students often ignore or are unaware of the <u>properties of words</u> and their role in achieving tone and style. The time for such concern occurs in the revision process, where the skillful writer can only benefit from an awareness of the choices available that rest in the properties that words possess. <u>Diction</u> involves the choice of the correct word for what one wants to communicate and is a matter of semantics. <u>Style</u> evolves from placing the right word in the right place according to the choices made as a matter of syntax and, ultimately, grammar. <u>Usage</u> also involves the correct word in the right place, a consideration beyond both diction and style that is a matter of social convention. Finally, words have an <u>etymology</u> or history, both diachronic and synchronic, and these choices stem from a consideration of semantics in terms of historical denotation and connotation. The richness of vocabulary in the English language, due especially but not limited to the Anglo-Saxon, Latin, French, and Norse influences, leads to problems for many writers because more than one word exists for each object, idea, and concept we wish to express. Unlike an artificial language such as mathematics, where each concept has but one symbol, natural language abounds in choices that require judicious selection. (See Chapters 23, 24, 25, in the <u>Handbook</u>.)

The best examples for classroom discussion of the concepts of diction and style do not necessarily come from the <u>Handbook</u> nor workbooks but from the writing produced by your own students. You may wish to maintain a special journal just for such entries centered on diction that you extract from student's essays as you evaluate them. Even though the sentences will be out of context, they can be presented to the class with an overhead projector or to collaborative groups as examples to comment upon.

Characteristics of Words

Alert your students to pay special attention to the various characteristics of words: <u>denotation</u> and <u>connotation</u> (Section 25c in the <u>Handbook</u>), <u>specific</u> and <u>general</u> (Section 25a), <u>concrete</u> and <u>abstract</u> (Section 25b), and the <u>usage levels</u> (Glossary of Usage). You may wish to refine and explain these properties somewhat.

Words, in terms of their literal (denotative) and associated (connotative) meanings, produce special effects on readers to such a degree that advertising copy and propaganda could not succeed without attention to them. Few words in our language merely name something; most imply a value judgment as well. If writers are aware of these associations, they can easily and deliberately affect the tone of their writing. It is when the writer loses sight of words' associative meanings, as in nonselective, injudicious use of a thesaurus, that problems arise.

Few among us would disagree on those characteristics of words described as general and specific. But the characteristics are relative. "Dress" is more specific than "garment," but "dress" is more general than "wedding dress." Attention to the rhetorical (audience and purpose) context should help students to select the degree of specificity desired, since selecting the specific word provides additional information and appeals to the imagination.

The dualities of concrete and abstract as characteristics of words are also worthy of attention. They usually are thought of in tandem with the dualities of specific and general. The concrete, specific characteristics of words usually receive favor because, perhaps, they best reflect the realities we see and know. But, for some purposes, the concrete, specific words are not necessarily the better choice over the abstract, general words. Writing in literary criticism, philosophy, and theology, to name but a few examples, requires a vocabulary for ideas and concepts that will tend toward the axis of abstract-general. Both concrete and abstract words exist to be used. Consider the following two groups.

I. It is difficult to understand his <u>bereavement</u>.

II. He is <u>lonely</u>.
He is <u>sad</u>.
He feels a <u>loss</u>.
He is <u>unhappy</u>.

Not one of the specific, concrete words in the second grouping conveys the meaning of the abstract word <u>bereavement</u>.

Usage Levels.

The <u>usage levels</u>, which can be thought of as "the good manners of language," are divisions of language use based on their appropriateness to certain audiences in certain places on certain occasions. One way to demonstrate this concept to students is to ask them to consider what differences occur in the language they speak in the following situations: the locker room after exercising, on the telephone describing last night's date to one's best friend, at home during dinner discussing the same date with your parents, or complaining about an essay grade to your friend as compared to complaining to your instructor. Using a comparison and contrast pattern of development, students can compose paragraphs from these or similar suggestions you make.

What students will discover is that certain characteristics of language tend to appear only during certain occasions with certain audiences, while other characteristics appear in all of them. The differences have been classified into many paradigms, but the following is indicative of general agreement:

Formal Literary English
Written Standard English
Colloquial English
Informal English

The appearance of the paradigm is not to be interpreted as representing either a hierarchy or a preference.

The writer selects language at each level to accomplish the task at hand. <u>Formal literary English</u> is a written form for serious, learned writing about literary theory, philosophy, economics, political science, and so forth. Jargon might be present that is appropriate to the subject matter or discipline of the writing. The <u>written standard</u> is less formal but, at the same time, not colloquial. It is the standard used in college essays and the world of trade and commerce. It lacks idioms, contractions, abbreviations, slang, gobbledygook, sexism, and jargon. <u>Colloquial English</u> is the grammatically correct spoken language of polite people and usually contains slang, clichés, idioms, and contractions. Informal English is the spoken variety that neglects grammatical accuracy, correct pronunciations, and, in addition to containing slang, clichés, idioms, and contractions, often includes vulgarisms.

Certain words in our language (e.g., the prepositions and conjunctions) appear in all four levels. The written standard and the formal literary levels share many words as do the colloquial and informal levels. Problems arise when students unwittingly use words and constructions from the informal and colloquial levels, less rarely from the formal level, in their writing. Chief among these will be idioms, clichés, slang, and colloquial words and phrases. (See the Handbook, Chapters 23, 24, and 25.)

Do not underestimate the value of the dictionary to students in making choices of diction. Although most students own or have access to a recently published college level dictionary, few know how to use it to its fullest advantage. Remind them to read the "front matter" in the dictionary, which explains the arrangement of the data in the entries, the labels applied to usage, the abbreviations used, and the principles underlying the definitions. Some dictionary publishers will, upon request, provide instructors with free guides for distribution to students that are designed to acquaint students with the wealth of information contained in their particular dictionary; however, the guides work well, with minor adjustments, with all currently available dictionaries.

We do not use words in writing in isolation; they each have a context or collocation. The words affect the context, and the context affects the words. The choices of words the writer selects affect the tone toward the reader or audience as well as the subject matter. As symbols of our experience and knowledge, our words convey meanings. The accuracy of our written communications depends very heavily on the way we choose and arrange these words. It is too important a part of the writing process to either overlook or treat cursorily.

Sexist and Other Biased Language

The last ten years or so, both within and beyond academe, have been marked by general concern over the use of sexist and other biased language. The Modern Writer's Handbook is among the very first to devote a full chapter to this subject. That this chapter should be required reading in your course can only benefit the student.

Biased language in reference to ethnic groups and nationalities has received appropriate attention in texts and classrooms during the past fifteen years. The language we use to refer to some groups, such as the disabled and the gays, has only recently been given careful consideration. For example, the terms "disabled" and "person with a disability" are now preferred to the older "handicap" and "handicapped person." As the Handbook points out in Chapter 24, words to designate some groups, such as American Indians, Afro-Americans, and gays, are in flux.

Recently, much concern has been expressed over the sexist language that has been inherited and passed on to us by previous generations. Recent psychological studies have revealed that women, on the whole, do, indeed, resent the use of the masculine markers in any form, noun or pronominal, to represent humankind. The key for our student writers, then, is to avoid all words and phrases that carry bias of any type. In order to do this, we as instructors must make our students aware of such bias when it occurs in their writing. To assist the instructor with this task, the guidelines developed by the National Council of Teachers of English are reprinted here, with permission.

Guidelines for Nonsexist Use of Language in NCTE Publications (Revised, 1985)

Introduction

During the 1971 Annual Convention of the National Council of Teachers of English in Las Vegas, Nevada, the Executive Committee and the Board of Directors approved the formation of an NCTE Committee on the Role and Image of Women in the Council and the Profession. As the result of a resolution passed by the members of NCTE at the 1974 Annual Convention, one of the committee's responsibilities was to assist in setting guidelines for nonsexist[1] use of language in NCTE publications.

Suggestions were elicited from editors of Council journals and from professional staff members at NCTE, as well as from members of the Women's Committee. Copies of the guidelines also went to all members of the Board of Directors. At the 1975 Annual Convention, the Board of Directors adopted a formal policy statement that read in part: "The National Council of Teachers of English should encourage the use of nonsexist language, particularly through its publications and periodicals."

---

[1] Although *nonsexist* is a word traditionally used to describe such language, other terms have come into common use, namely, *gender-neutral, sex-fair, gender-free.*

Ten years have passed since these guidelines were created, and although language usage has begun to change, the importance of the guidelines has not diminished. Because language plays a central role in the way human beings think and behave, we still need to promote language that opens rather than closes possibilities for women and men. Whether teaching in the classroom, assigning texts, determining curriculum, serving on national committees, or writing in professional publications, NCTE members directly and indirectly influence thought and behavior.

As an educational publisher, NCTE is not alone in its concern for fair treatment of men and women. The role of education is to make choices available, not to limit opportunities. Censorship removes possibilities; these guidelines extend what is available by offering alternatives to traditional usages and to editorial choices that restrict meaning.

Language

This section deals primarily with word choice. Many of the examples are matters of vocabulary; a few are matters of grammatical choice. The vocabulary items are relatively easy to deal with, since the English lexicon has a history of rapid change. Grammar is a more difficult area, and we have chosen to use alternatives that already exist in the language rather than to invent new constructions. In both cases, recommended alternatives have been determined by what is graceful and unobstructive. The purpose of these changes is to suggest alternative styles.

Generic "*Man*"

1. Since the word *man* has come to refer almost exclusively to adult males, it is sometimes difficult to recognize its generic meaning.

Problems	*Alternatives*
mankind	humanity, human beings, people[2]
man's achievements	human achievements
the best man for the job	the best person for the job, the best man or woman for the job
man-made	synthetic, manufactured, crafted, machine-made
the common man	the average person, ordinary people
cavemen	cave dwellers, prehistoric people

2. Sometimes the combining form -*woman* is used alongside -*man* in occupational terms and job titles, but we prefer using the same titles for men and women when naming jobs that could be held by both. Note, too, that using the same forms for men and women is a way to avoid using the combining form -person as a substitute for -*woman* only.

Problems	*Alternatives*
chairman/chairwoman	chair, coordinator (of a committee or department), moderator (of a meeting), presiding officer, head, chairperson
businessman/businesswoman	business executive or manager
congressman/congresswoman	congressional representative
policeman/policewoman	police officer
salesman/saleswoman	sales clerk, sales representative, salesperson

---

[2] A one-word substitution for *mankind* isn't always possible, especially in set phrases like the story of *mankind*. Sometimes recasting the sentence altogether may be the best solution.

fireman	fire fighter
mailman	letter carrier

Generic "*He*" and "*His*"

Because there is no one pronoun in English that can be effectively substituted for *he* or *his*, we offer several alternatives. The forms *he or she* has been the NCTE house style over the last ten years, on the premise that it is less distracting than *she or her* or *he/she*. There are other choices, however. The one you make will depend on what you are writing.

1. Sometimes it is possible to drop the possessive form *his* altogether or to substitute an article.

Problems	*Alternatives*
The average student is worried about his grades.	The average student is worried about grades.
When the student hands in his paper, read it immediately	When the student hands in the paper, read it immediately.

2. Often, it makes sense to use the plural instead of the singular.

Problems	*Alternatives*
Give the student his grade right away.	Give the students their grades right away.
Ask the student to hand in his work as soon as he is finished.	Ask students to hand in their work as soon as they are finished.

3. The first or second person can sometimes be substituted for the third person.

Problems	*Alternatives*
As a teacher, he is faced daily with the problem of paperwork.	As teachers, we are faced daily with the problem of paperwork.
When a teacher asks his students for an evaluation, he is putting himself on the spot.	When you ask your students for an evaluation, you are putting yourself on the spot.

4. In some situations, the pronoun *one* (*one's*) can be substituted for *he* (*his*), but it should be used sparingly. Notice that the use of *one*--like the use of *we* or *you*--changes the tone of what you are writing.

Problems	*Alternatives*
He might well wonder what his response should be.	One might well wonder what one's response should be.

5. A sentence with *he* or *his* can sometimes be recast in the passive voice or another impersonal construction.

Problems	*Alternatives*
Each student should hand in his paper promptly.	Papers should be handed in promptly.
He found such an idea intolerable.	Such an idea was intolerable.

6. When the subject is an indefinite pronoun, the plural form *their* can occasionally be used with it, especially when the referent for the pronoun is clearly understood to be plural.

Problems	*Alternatives*
When everyone contributes his	When everyone contributes their

own ideas, the discussion will
be a success.

own ideas, the discussion will
be a success.

But since this usage is transitional, it is usually better to recast the sentence and avoid the indefinite pronoun.

Problems

When everyone contributes his
own ideas, the discussion will
be a success.

Alternatives

When all the students contribute
their own ideas, the discussion
will be a success.

7. Finally, sparing use can be made of *he* or *she* and *his* or *her*. It is best to restrict this choice to contexts in which the pronouns are not repeated.

Problems

Each student will do better if he
has a voice in the decision.

Each student can select his
own topic.

Alternatives

Each student will do better if he or
she has a voice in the decision.

Each student can select his or her
own topic.

Sex-Role Stereotyping

Word choices sometimes reflect unfortunate and unconscious assumptions about sex roles--for example, that farmers are always men and elementary school teachers are always women; that men are valued for their accomplishments and women for their physical attributes; or that men are strong and brave while women are weak and timid. We need to examine the assumptions inherent in certain stock phrases and choose nonstereotyped alternatives.

1. Identify men and women in the same way. Diminutive or special forms to name women are usually unnecessary. In most cases, generic terms such as *doctor* or *actor* should be assumed to include both men and women. Only occasionally are alternate forms needed, and in these cases, the alternate form replaces both the masculine and the feminine titles.

Problems

stewardess

authoress
waitress
poetess
coed
lady lawyer
male nurse

Alternatives

flight attendant (for both *steward*
     and *stewardess*)
author
server, food server
poet
student
lawyer . . . she
nurse . . . he

2. Do not represent women as occupying only certain jobs or roles and men as occupying only certain others.

Problems

the kindergarten teacher . . . she

the principal . . . he

Have your mother send a snack
  for the party.

NCTE convention goers and their

Alternatives

occasionally use the kindergarten
     teacher . . . he
     or kindergarten teachers . . . they
Occasionally use the principal . . . she
     or principals . . . they
Have a parent send a snack
  for the party.
occasionally use Have your father . . .
     or Have your parents . . . .
NCTE convention goers and their

wives are invited.	spouses are invited.
Writers become so involved in their work that they neglect their wives and children.	Writers become so involved in their work that they neglect their families.

3. Treat men and women in a parallel manner.

Problems	*Alternatives*
The class interviewed Chief Justice Burger and Mrs. O'Connor.	The class interviewed Warren Burger and Sandra O'Connor.
	or . . . Mr. Burger and Ms. O'Connor.
	or. . . Chief Justice Burger and Justice O'Connor.
The reading list included Proust, Joyce, Gide, and Virginia Woolf.	The reading list included Proust, Joyce, Gide, and Woolf.
	or. . . Marcel Proust, James Joyce, Andre Gide, and Virginia Woolf.
Both Bill Smith, a straight-A sophomore, and Kathy Ryan, a pert junior, won writing awards.	Both sophomore Bill Smith, a straight-A student, and junior Kathy Ryan, editor of the school paper, won writing awards.

4. Seek alternatives to language that patronizes or trivializes women, as well as to language that reinforces stereotyped images of both women and men.

Problems	*Alternatives*
The president of the company hired a gal Friday.	The president of the company hired an assistant.
I'll have my girl do it.	I'll ask my secretary to do it.
Stella is a career woman.	Stella is a professional *or* Stella is a doctor (architect, etc.).
The ladies on the committee all supported the bill.	The women on the committee all supported the bill.
Pam had lunch with the girls from the office.	Pam had lunch with the women from the office.
This is a man-sized job.	This is a big (huge, enormous) job.
That's just an old wives' tale.	That's just a superstition (superstitious story).
Don't be such an old lady.	Don't be so fussy.

Sexist Language in a Direct Quotation

Quotations cannot be altered, but there are other ways of dealing with this problem.

1. Avoid the quotation altogether if it is not really necessary.

2. Paraphrase the quotation, giving the original author credit for the idea.

3. If the quotation is fairly short, recast it as an indirect quotation, substituting nonsexist words as necessary.

Problems	*Alternatives*
Among the questions asked by the school representatives was the following: "Considering the	Among the questions asked by the school representatives was one about what degree of knowledge

ideal college graduate, what degree of knowledge would you prefer him to have in each of the curricular areas?"

the ideal college graduate should have in each of the curricular areas.

Sample Revised Passage

Substantial revisions or deletions are sometimes necessary when problems overlap or when stereotyped assumptions about men and women so pervade a passage that simple replacement of words is inadequate.

Problems	*Alternatives*
Each student who entered the classroom to find himself at the mercy of an elitist, Vassar-trained Miss Fidditch could tell right away that the semester would be a trial. The trend in composition pedagogy toward student-centered essays and away form hours of drill on grammatical correctness has meant, at least for him, that he can finally learn to write. But Macrorie, Elbow, and Janet Emig could drive the exasperated teacher of a cute and perky cheerleader type to embrace the impersonal truth of <u>whom</u> as direct object rather than fight his way against the undertow of a gush of personal experience. As Somerset Maugham remarked, "Good prose should resemble the conversations of a well-bred man," and both Miss Fidditch and the bearded guru who wants to "get inside your head" must realize it.	The trend in composition pedagogy toward student-centered essays, represented by such writers as Ken Macrorie, Peter Elbow, and Janet Emig, has meant that some students are finally learning to write. Yet the movement away from hours of drill on grammatical correctness has brought with it a new problem: in the hands of the inexperienced teacher, student essays can remain little more than unedited piles of personal experiences and emotions.

Representation of Men and Women

Important as language is, striving for nonsexist usage is to little purpose if the underlying assumptions about men and women continue to restrict them to traditional roles. If women never enter an author's world, for example, it little avails a writer or editor to refer scrupulously to students as "they" and prehistoric people as "cave dwellers." Thus, teachers and other professionals must be alert to the possible sexist implications of the content as well as the language of educational materials.

It has been enhartening to note that in the last ten years, trade publishers, textbook publishers, and publishers of reference works have become acutely aware of sexist language, thus largely alleviating the problem of discriminatory reference. Still, vigilance must be exercised.

The following recommendations concerning educational materials are made to correct traditional omissions of women or perpetuations of stereotypes.

Booklists

71

1. Items for a booklist should be chosen to emphasize the equality of men and women and to show them in nontraditional as well as traditional roles. Many children's favorites and classics may contain sexist elements, but books that are valuable for other reasons should not be excluded. The annotations, however, should be written in nonsexist language.
2. Picture books should be chosen showing males and females actively participating in a variety of situations at home, work, and play.
3. Booklists should be organized by subject headings that do not assume stereotyped male and female interests.

Problems	*Alternatives*
Books for Boys	Arts and Crafts
Books for Girls	Sports
	Travel

Teaching Units

1. The topic and organization of teaching units should be carefully considered to avoid sexist implications. Literature by and about both women and men should be included whenever possible.

2. When materials are chosen that present stereotyped assumptions about men and women, they should be balanced by other materials that show nontraditional roles and assumptions. *Jemima Puddle-Duck* and *Peter Rabbit* read together, for instance, show foolishness is not a sex-linked characteristic. Vera Brittain's *A Testament of Youth* and Ernest Hemingway's *The Sun Also Rises* present the aftermath of World War I from provocative perspectives. Placing a book in the proper historical context and using discussion questions that reflect an awareness of the sexist elements are good strategies.
3. Activities suggested in teaching units should not be segregated by sex: Boys can make costumes and girls can build sets.

Reference Books and Research Materials

Reference books can be implicitly sexist in their titles, organizations, content and language. Editors of such books should follow the suggestions in this publication to ensure nonsexist language in bibliographies, indexes, style manuals, and teacher's guides. In research works, if both males and females were studied, references to individual subjects should not assume that they are all one sex.

Implementation of Guidelines

These guidelines for nonsexist language are suggestions for teachers, writers, and contributors to NCTE publications. For the editors of NCTE publications, however, they are a statement of editorial policy.

Traditionally, editors have set the style for their publications--deciding, for example, whether there should be a comma before the conjunction in a series or whether the first item in a list after a colon should begin with a capital letter. Style decisions have sometimes been made in response to public pressure. Writing *Negro* with a capital letter instead of a lowercase letter and, later, using *black* instead of *Negro* were both style decisions of this sort for many publishing houses, newspapers, and magazines.

It is an editor's job to rewrite whenever necessary to eliminate awkward language, inconsistency, or inaccuracy. If a job title is inaccurately identified in an article as

Director of Public Instruction but the title is actually Supervisor of Public Instruction, the editor changes the wording as a matter of course and without asking the author's approval. If the subject matter or tone of an article is totally inappropriate for the particular publication, it would also be the editor's prerogative to return the manuscript to the author. In the case of language inconsistent with the guidelines, it is the editor's duty to question the author's use of a particular term; on the other hand, the author has the right to insist on its use, but a footnote will be provided to reflect such insistence.

The choices suggested in these guidelines are intended as additions to the style sheets and manuals already in use.

References

Authors and editors who would like to see further suggestions for creating a graceful, nondiscriminatory writing style should refer to these publications. (Note that many of the publishers' guidelines are in the process of being revised.)

American Psychological Association Task Force on Issues of Sexual Bias in Graduate Education. "Guidelines for Nonsexist Use of Language." *American Psychologist* 30 (June 1975): 682-84.

Editorial and Art Content Criteria for Treatment of Minorities and Women. Lexington: Ginn and Company. (Available from the publisher, 191 Spring Street, Lexington, MA 02173.)

Fairness in Educational Materials: Exploring the Issues. Chicago: Science Research Associates, Inc. (Available from the publisher, 15 North Wacker Drive, Chicago, Il 60606.)

Guidelines for Bias-Free Publishing. New York: McGraw-Hill Book Company. (Available from the publisher's distribution center, Princeton Road, Hightstown, NJ 08520.)

Guidelines for Creating Positive Sexual and Racial Images in Educational Materials. New York: Macmillan Publishing Company, 1975. (Available in limited quantities from the publisher, 866 Third Avenue, New York, NY 10022.)

Guidelines for Developing Bias-Free Instructional Materials. Morristown: Silver Burdett Company, 1979. (Available from the publisher, 250 James Street, Morristown, NJ 07960.)

Guidelines for the Development of Elementary and Secondary Instructional Materials. New York: Holt, Rinehart and Winston School Department, 1975. (Available from the publisher, 383 Madison Avenue, New York, NY 10017.)

Miller, Casey, and Kate Swift. *The Handbook of Nonsexist Writing: For Writers Editors and Speakers.* New York: Barnes and Noble Books, 1980. (Available from Harper and Row, 10 East 53rd Street, New York, NY 10022.)

Nilsen, Alleen Pace. "Editing for Sex," *Idaho English Journal* 6 (Spring 1983): 12+.

_____. "Winning the Great *He/She* Battle." *College English* 46 (February 1984): 151.

Statement on Bias-Free Materials. New York: Association of America Publishers. (Available from AAP, One Park Avenue, New York, NY 10016.)

Works Cited

Graves, Richard L. "Levels of Skill in the Composing Process." The Writing Teacher's Sourcebook. 3rd ed. Gary Tate, Edward P. J. Corbett, and Nancy Myers, eds. New York: Oxford UP, 1988. 193-98.

Sudol, Ronald A. Revising: New Essays for Teachers of Writing. Urbana, IL: NCTE, 1982.

Weathers, Winston. "Teaching Style: A Possible Anatomy." <u>The Writing Teacher's Sourcebook</u>, 3rd ed. Gary Tate Edward and P. J. Corbett, and Nancy Myers, eds. New York: Oxford UP, 1988. 187-92.

For Further Reading

To initiate your study of **Revision**, you might begin with Ronald Sudol's book <u>Revising: New Essays for Teachers of Writing</u> (Urbana, IL: NCTE, 1982), which covers practical teaching methods as well as theoretical issues in the study of revising. For a practical guide to revising, try Richard Lanham's <u>Revising Prose</u>, 3rd ed. (New York: Macmillan, 1992), which comes with a self-teaching exercise book. See also Edward Klonoski, "Using the Eyes of the PC to Teach Revision" (<u>Computers and Composition</u> 11 [1994]: 71-78) and Linda Flower and John R. Hayes, "Problem-Solving Strategies and the Writing Process" (<u>College English</u> 39 [1977]: 442-48).

Sentence Combining has similarly been discussed in the literature from both a research and a pedagogical perspective. Important research on sentence combining began with transformational grammarians: the seminal study by Kellogg Hunt, <u>Grammatical Structures Written at Three Grade Levels</u> (NCTE Research Report #3, 1965) followed by Frank O'Hare's <u>Sentence Combining: Improving Student Writing Without Formal Grammar Instruction</u> (NCTE Research Report #15, 1973). Teaching books include Daiker, Kerek, and Morenberg's <u>Sentence Combining and the Teaching of Writing</u> (Carbondale: Southern Illinois UP, 1985), and William Strong's <u>Sentence Combining and Paragraph Building</u> (New York: Random, 1981).

Some good resources on **style** include Richard Lanham, <u>Analyzing Prose</u> (New York: Scribner's, 1983); Winston Weathers, <u>An Alternate Style: Options in Composition</u> (Rochelle Park, NJ: Hayden, 1980); Joseph Williams, <u>Style: Ten Lessons in Clarity and Grace</u>, 3rd ed. (Glenview: Scott-Foresman, 1989), and I. Hashimoto, "Sentence Variety: Where Theory and Practice Meet and Lose" (<u>Composition Studies</u> 21 [1993]: 66-77).

To learn more about **composition and gender** you might begin with Dennis Baron <u>Grammar and Gender</u> (New Haven: Yale UP, 1986), Francine Frank, et al., <u>Language, Gender, and Professional Writing: Theoretical Approaches and Guidelines for Nonsexist Usage</u> (New York: MLA, 1989); or Casey Miller and Kate Swift, <u>The Handbook of Non-Sexist Writing</u>, 2nd ed. (New York: Harper, 1988), or Deborah Tannen, <u>Gender and Discourse</u> (New York: Oxford UP, 1995). To learn about differences in men's and women's speech, read the lively and interesting new best-seller by Deborah Tannen, You Just Don't Understand: Women and Men in Conversation (New York: Ballentine, 1990).

CHAPTER 8. EDITING

We have discussed rewriting as an essential stage in the writing process, one in which the writer re-sees the text and rethinks what is written and how--a process which we have called revision. Another aspect of rewriting involves editing to improve the surface features of the text: making corrections in grammar, usage, and mechanics. As Jeanette Harris points out, "many of our students fail to detect surface errors in their compositions because . . . they see what they mean rather than what they write" (464). She reminds us that proofreading to detect errors involves reading skill as well as writing skill, and that students need to learn to read differently at the editing stage--to deliberately "counteract the 'normal' process of reading . . . so that they see what is actually on the page rather than what they expect to see" (465).

Editing, not to be confused with revising, can enter the writing process at any time. But editing is not considered a function of prewriting or of revising. Editing can probably be most beneficial if it occurs after some re-vision has taken place. Editing involves grammar, mechanics, and format: micro-level changes that contribute to the essay's overall structure, development, tone, sense of audience, emphasis, unity, and coherence. It can be thought of as the "fixing" or "fine-tuning" of paragraphs, sentences, and words after they have been revised or "re-seen" on the macro-level.

Instructors can provide some useful guidelines to assist students with the editing process. First and foremost, you will probably need to stress that the concerns of grammar, mechanics, and format do not really belong to the revising stage in the process. As noted earlier, the primary concerns of revision are macro-level changes involving overall essay organization: the introduction, the conclusion, the body; adding, deleting, changing, and rearranging content; changes within paragraphs and within sentences; and choices of words. Too often, students only edit and think they have revised.

Checking the grammar, punctuation, mechanics, and format for accuracy are important parts of the writing process properly assigned to the categories of editing and proofreading. These two terms can be used synonymously since their differences are really of a recursive nature; that is, a writer edits, then proofs to ascertain that all is correct. If not, one is led back to editing, and the proofreading begins anew.

Grammar, Punctuation, and Mechanics

Recommend that students edit for each category, one at a time, which will mean at least three readings of the draft at a minimum: for grammar, punctuation, and mechanics-format. Some teachers recommend with success that the essay be read backwards, word for word. This methodology often helps writers who have problems with spelling, punctuation, the passive voice, overuse of the forms of <u>to be</u>, dangling modifiers, and so forth. This procedure will not be as successful in checking for the presence and appropriateness of transition words and/or phrases. Instead, a reminder to read each paragraph, beginning to end, to check only the transition markers should suffice. Remind the students to consult the complete checklist for editing and proofreading in Section 3e of the <u>Handbook.</u>

Other useful techniques for editing practice include group work, either in peer groups or involving the class as a whole, in which students comment on a text displayed on an overhead projection. The instructor should say as little as possible, reserving commentary for when the group session appears to be slowing down. Students can learn much from observing how their peers approach the tasks of editing and proofing.

Students may keep a special journal, another device that helps in the editing-proofreading process. Begun after receiving the evaluation of the first essay, the student records and classifies in the journal each of the grammatical, mechanical, and format errors that appears in the first and the successively evaluated essays. The student then consults the individualized log of errors each time she or he performs the editing-proofreading process, and searches the text, hopefully to eliminate any recurrences of the same types of errors. In some writing programs, this device has been formalized as an "essay evaluation folder," which the instructor collects periodically to ensure that students are keeping their "error logs" current.

Those students who use the computer for their writing most likely will seek your advice about the use and value of commercially produced software packages billed as style and spelling checkers. Most of the "style checker" computer programs do contain features of interest and use for students, especially those that have a concordance construction capability. Students can, for example, readily scan a concordance of their essays to check the number of times various forms of the verb <u>to be</u> and the personal pronoun <u>I</u> occur and edit accordingly. Because many style programs cater to the communication expectations of the business community, the student may receive advice about style that is not in accord with your expectations. For example, a style program may inform the author that 82 percent of the sentences contain more than ten words and recommend that half of them be shortened. Spelling checkers also serve useful functions, but students need to be aware of their limitations. These programs cannot differentiate between the correct usage of homonyms, for example. If a student confuses <u>its</u> with <u>it's</u>, whose with who's, or there, their, they're, the program is of no help, nor can it detect typographical errors where from appears as form or made appears as make.

It is perhaps less beneficial to students for an instructor to adopt an evaluatory criterion that X (select any number from three to ten) grammatical, punctuation, or format errors result in a failing grade for the essay. Students do not deliberately make such errors, and little can be gained by adding to the tension these students may experience when writing. But you may want to mention this fact to your students to impress upon them the importance of the editing and proofreading process. In place of threats of failure, show students how to seek out and find patterns of errors in their writing and provide advice, with the help of the Handbook, to overcome the errors.

Computer Editing

The same features of computer software programs that help writers to compose, draft, and revise can also help writers to edit their texts. Using the standard features of most word-processing functions (insert, delete, cut, paste, move, search, and spell check), your students may add new information, delete unneeded words and phrases (or even sentences), rearrange words within a sentence, substitute one word for another, locate specific words and phrases that they wish to change, and correct spelling.

In addition to standard word-processing features, other software programs are available that may help your students to edit their work, making it both clearer and more direct. Such programs, variously called text-editing or style-checking programs, have pluses and minuses for writers. Text-editing programs prove beneficial insofar as they can help writers to expand their horizons, to see alternatives for varying sentence structures; for example, or to encourage a writer to choose a wider vocabulary. If a writer habitually uses a cliched phrase such as in order to when the more direct to would serve better, the text-editing program may point out this phrase to the writer, who then may choose to avoid the cliche. Or perhaps a writer tends to write in a series of simple sentences; the text-editing program may tell the writer the proportion of simple to compound/complex sentences, thus providing the writer with new insights into his or her writing style.

However, students often do not realize that the suggestions and analyses provided by text-editors cannot be relied on completely. Such programs only examine certain, often limited, surface features of a text; they cannot understand what the text is saying. So the writer must ultimately take responsibility for the text and for deciding whether or not the computer's advice is worth following. Another misconception about text-editors is that they "check grammar." Although most analysis programs can provide information about the number of words or the average length of words in texts, they are incapable of any sophisticated grammatical analyses and thus cannot tell a writer, for example, whether the commas are used correctly or whether the verb tenses are correct. Some programs can identify certain mechanical errors such as unbalanced quotation marks or parentheses, or missing capital letters at the beginning of a sentence. However, we need to be certain to remind our students that text-editing programs cannot improve the correctness of a text; only writers can do that.

Works Cited

Harris, Jeanette. "Proofreading: A Reading/Writing Skill." College Composition and Communication 38 (1987) 464-65.

PART III. ASSIGNING AND ASSESSING

CHAPTER 9. DESIGNING WRITING ASSIGNMENTS

Many years ago, Wayne C. Booth delivered a speech to the Illinois Council of College Teachers of English titled "Boring from Within: The Art of the Freshman Essay" (1963). Booth pointed out in his presentation that much of the writing done by our students was uninteresting and dull; and furthermore, that if the writing bored the teacher, the teaching was sure to fail. Booth says "As I try to sort out the various possible cures for those batches of boredom--in ink, double-spaced, on one side of the sheet, only, please--I find them falling into three groups: efforts to give the students a sharper sense of writing to an audience, efforts to give them some substance to express, and efforts to improve their habits of observation and of approach to their task--what might be called improving their mental personalities."

In summary, what Booth was calling for was a "rhetorical" approach to writing assignments: one that takes into account the knowledge, personality, and intentions of the writer on a subject as well as the needs and expectations of the audience. To make good writing assignments takes planning and effort on the part of the teacher to help the students see the rhetorical context for their writing. An assignment should be a "careful blend of the old and the new" (Williams 237). A teacher should consider a sequence of assignments that builds on what students already know and specifies the writing skills that are expected with each writing task.

Erika Lindemann includes a "Heuristic for Designing Writing Assignments" that you may find particularly useful:

A Heuristic for Designing Writing Assignments

1. *What do I want the students to do*? Is it worth doing? Why? What will the assignment tell me about what they've learned? How does it fit my objectives to this point in the course? Does the assignment assess what students can *do* or what

they *know*? Am I relating their work to the real world (including academic settings) or only to my class or the text? Does the assignment require specialized knowledge? Does it appeal to the interests and experiences of my students?

2. *How do I want students to do the assignment*? Are students working alone or together? In what ways will they practice prewriting, writing, and rewriting? Are writing, reading, speaking, and listening reinforcing each other? Have I given students enough information to make effective choices about the subject, purpose, form, and mode?

3. *For whom are students writing*? Who is the audience? Do students have enough information to assume a role with respect to the audience?

4. *When will students do the assignment*? How does the assignment relate to what comes before and after it in the course? Is the assignment sequenced to give enough time for prewriting, writing, and rewriting? How much time inside and outside of class will students need for each stage? To what extent will I guide students' work? What deadlines do I want to set for the collection of students' papers (or various stages of the project)?

5. *What will I do with the assignment*? How will I evaluate the work? What constitutes a "successful" response to the assignment? Will other students or the writer have a say in evaluating the paper? What problems did I encounter when I wrote my paper on this assignment? How can the assignment be improved?

A student's writing assignment begins with the teacher's initial conception of it. How well students succeed in meeting a teacher's expectations when writing usually bears a direct relationship to how well-planned and thought-through the assignments are before they are announced. Prior to the beginning of the course you may wish to plan and assign a sequence to the writing assignments based on one or more objectives that reflect your philosophy of composition and that take into account the cognitive and/or affective domains. You may also wish to establish policies for prompt submission of all writing assignments, not just final products, and for whatever penalties ensue when these expectations are not met.

Cognitive and Affective Domains

While much of what writing teachers do in the classroom and in conferences centers on the writing process, and evidence of its use is expected and hopefully reflected in students' writing assignments, the writing process leads to a product that communicates something. What it communicates reflects the cognitive and/or affective domains of the writer's intellect. Bearing these domains in mind, then, you can devise writing assignments in a manner that makes them easier for students to write and easier for you to evaluate, especially if you inform the students of the rationale underlying the assignment. Some suggested writing assignments follow the explanation of the domains that follow.

The processes of perception, memory, judgment, and reasoning contribute to the cognitive domain whereas emotion and feeling characterize the affective domain. Borrowing from Kratwohl, Bloom, and Masia's Taxonomy of Educational Objectives: Handbook II, we can arrange the categories of the cognitive domain in the ascending format of a ladder, which is read from left to right, bottom to top.

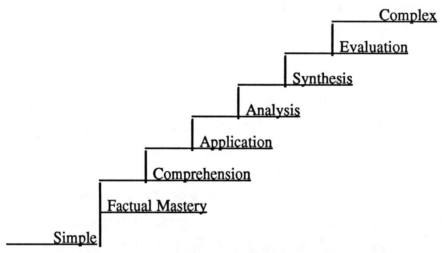

The model purports to visualize the objectives within the cognitive domain in terms of "the recall or recognition of knowledge and the development of intellectual abilities and skills" (Bloom et al. 7). An acquaintance with the following cognitive objectives can help you plan the cognitive level of your writing assignments (Kratwohl et al. 186-93):

Factual Mastery: "The recall of specific facts" (186).

Comprehension: "The lowest level of understanding." "One knows what is being communicated and can make use of the material or idea being communicated without necessarily relating it to other material or seeing its fullest implications" (190).

Application: "Use of abstractions (general ideas, rules of procedure, or generalized methods, technical principles, ideas, theories) in particular and concrete situations" (191).

Analysis: "Breakdown of communication into its constituent elements or parts such that the relative hierarchy of ideas is made clear and/or relations between the ideas expressed are made explicit" (191).

Synthesis: "The putting together of elements and parts so as to form a whole. Arranging and combining the pieces, parts, elements, etc. in such a way as to constitute a pattern of structure not clearly there before" (192).

Evaluation: "Judgments about the value of material and methods for given purposes." "Use of a standard of appraisal" (193).

Movement from each step on the ladder of objectives from simple to complex assumes that the objectives of the previous step have been met. For example, an analysis paper, well done, will contain evidence not only of the objectives for analysis but also of those for application, comprehension, and factual mastery. On the one hand, few writing teachers would assign an essay with the objective of factual mastery in mind when a quiz would serve the purpose much more efficiently. On the other hand, an essay with comprehension as its objective will readily reveal whether or not the student author has achieved factual mastery of the topic.

Suggestions for the application of the cognitive objectives to actual writing assignments could take the following forms:

Factual Mastery: An objective description, as opposed to an impressionistic one of a person, place, or thing, or activity.

Comprehension: An objective description that reveals an understanding of a person, place, thing, or activity by at least naming its parts and the place of the whole in reality or the imagination.

Application: An objective description that reveals an understanding of a person, place, thing, or activity by not only naming its parts but knowing their utility or process.

Analysis: An objective description that reveals an understanding of a person, place, thing, or activity by naming its parts, their utility, and a statement of the organizational principle that creates a whole from the parts: a tearing-down. (The whole, then, is equal to the sum of its parts plus the principle of organization.)

Synthesis: The application of analysis: an objective description of a person, place, thing, or activity that names its parts, their principle of organization, and how they work together to form a whole—a building-up.

Evaluation: An objective evaluation, positive or negative, on the synthesis in the previous step: the person, place, thing, or activity does or does not do what it is supposed to do or expected to do with reasons to support one's judgment.

Some Sample Topics:

Persons: parents, police officer, rock star, athlete, drug dealer, minister, teacher, electrician, barber. Places: writing class, kitchen, bus stop, theater, church, registrar's office, police station, locker room. <u>Things</u>: tree, doll, train, pencil, book, basketball, computer, apartment, street lamp, glass of water. <u>Activities</u>: fire, walking, registering for classes, singing, swimming, riding a bicycle, playing a musical instrument, analyzing plot in a drama or novel.

A model also exists for the internalization of affective outcomes, "those objectives which emphasize a feeling tone, an emotion, or a degree of acceptance or rejection . . . expressed as interests, attitudes, appreciation, values, and emotional sets or biases" (Krathwohl et al. 7). Also arranged as a ladder and read in a similar manner as the previous model, the categories include (Krathwohl et al. 176-84):

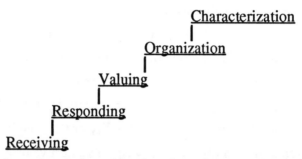

<u>Receiving</u>: One is "sensitized to the existence of certain phenomena and stimuli" (176). This category includes <u>awareness</u>, "to take into account without assessment" (177), <u>willingness</u>, "to tolerate, not to avoid" and "suspended judgment" (177), and <u>attentiveness</u>, "differentiation from competing stimuli" (178). In terms of a writing assignment, the affective outcome would be realized in an objective, noncommittal response to the topic.

<u>Responding</u>: "low level commitment . . . a step beyond reception" (178). It includes <u>acquiescence</u>, "obedience and compliance" . . . a response made "without fully accepting the reason for doing so" (179), <u>willingness</u>, a "voluntary" response, free choice, "assent, consent" (179), and <u>satisfaction</u>, an "emotional response: pleasure, zest, enjoyment" (179). A writing assignment with this outcome in mind would stress one of the three subcategories in terms of the response to the topic.

<u>Valuing</u>: "A thing, phenomenon, or behavior has worth . . . an attitude, a value" (180). This category subdivides into <u>acceptance</u>, "ascribing worth . . . belief" (181), <u>preference</u>, "pursue a value, to seek it out, to want it" (181), and <u>commitment</u>, "conviction . . . faith . . . loyalty" (182). An affective response on this level would contain evidence of "receiving" and "responding" as well as "value," the latter reflected in the force of the value: acceptance, preference, or commitment.

Organization: "Organization of values into a system . . . determining their interrelationships . . . establishing the dominant and persuasive ones" (182). Involved are two subdivisions: <u>conceptualization of a value</u>, "how the value relates to those" already held "or to new ones that one is coming to hold" (183); and <u>organization of a value system</u>, "to bring together a complex of values, possibly disparate, and to bring these into a ordered relationship with one another . . . to formulate a philosophy of life" (183). Writing at this level reflects how the values attributed to a topic relate to other values, old and new, and how they do or do not form a system.

Characterization: "Organization of values into some kind of internally consistent system," which results in acting consistently in accordance with the values . . . internalized" (184).

Writing assignments in a composition course or any course for that matter can be designed, then, to center on the cognitive domain or the affective domain or combinations of the two.

Sequencing Assignments

Effective writing assignments do not exist in isolation from each other. Their purpose is to realize the cognitive and affective outcomes through which all of us become educated. In addition effective writing assignments benefit the student most when sequenced in a manner that builds upon mastery of both skills and the cognitive/affective outcomes.

Sequencing your writing assignments requires careful planning before the course begins. Some writing programs provide you with a listing of the kinds of expository writing that students must produce. In such cases, simply devise a sequential order for the assignments if one does not already exist. In those cases where no such paradigm is readily available, you have a number of options from which to select.

Naturally, the <u>writing process</u> (prewriting, drafting, revising, editing, and proofreading), which is not linear per se, underlies and undergirds any type of sequential order for writing assignments. A number of sequencing options exist. One way to plan your assignments involves the rhetorical modes of discourse. One might begin by assigning a personal narrative, then move to description, classification, comparison and contrast, analogy, definition, example and illustration, process, cause and effect, and conclude the course with argument.

Beginning with a <u>personal narrative</u> wins favor from many instructors because, since the content springs from the student's memory of an experience, the question of "rightness" and "wrongness" of content does not enter. But other instructors, despite the arrangement of many texts that place personal narrative at the beginning of the book, believe that this kind of writing, well done, is too sophisticated and opt instead to begin with description or not to use sequencing by the modes of discourse at all.

We need, then, to be careful not to underestimate the difficulty of the personal essay assignment for students. Often teachers think that because the subject is one students are familiar with (themselves), somehow the assignment is easy. On the contrary, writing personal essays is a very demanding rhetorical task for the writer. As Williams points out, "it is extremely difficult to write on the implicit level, and unless you've attempted to convey a message solely through the narrative interaction of people and events, you may not fully appreciate just how hard it is" (245). To teach personal essay writing takes an investment of time that teachers may want to think about seriously.

Moving next to objective description, the student simply describes a person, place, thing, or activity, and empirical validation of the description determines the success of the writing. If the student subjectively describes a mood, feeling, or impression, the writing will hopefully re-create the mood, feeling, or impression or, at least, an understanding of it for the reader. The skills gained by writing description lead to classification, which takes its basis from the ability to compare things. This, in turn, leads logically to comparison and contrast and the latter's subclass of analogy. To build upon these, you could next assign definition, which includes the skills of description, classification, comparison, and contrast. Moving from the static to the dynamic, one then assigns process analysis which incorporates the earlier mastered skills and leads naturally to cause and effect. With these writing skills coupled to a formal study of critical thinking, your students are ready to write arguments. You need not necessarily assign an essay written in each of these modes. Some or all of the modes can be practiced at the level of the paragraph.

Many teachers find it helpful to require students to append a brief paragraph-by-paragraph description of their essays. For example:

Paragraph 1: Thesis and introduction

Paragraph 2: Definition and description

Paragraph 3: Classification and comparison

Paragraph 4: Analogy and examples

Paragraph 5: Comparison

Paragraph 6: Contrast

Paragraph 7: Conclusion

Such descriptions benefit both the student and the teacher-evaluator.

Another way to plan your sequencing of writing assignments is to base the sequence on either the cognitive or affective domains or both (see Section 9A in this

Guide). After an assignment geared to factual mastery and comprehension, simply add another rung on the cognitive ladder to each subsequent assignment. Or, as appropriate, use the model of the affective domain. After devising an assignment that will reveal the writer's awareness, willingness, and attentiveness to receiving, consider devising one based on response that will reveal the presence or absence of acquiescence, willingness, and satisfaction. The objectives that characterize the "internalization" of affective outcomes can also be recognized in writing assignments sequenced on the model of the rhetorical modes.

Still another option for sequencing your writing assignments relates to the communication triangle discussed in Chapter 1 of this Guide. Borrowing and adapting from James Kinneavy's A Theory of Discourse (1971), you can sequence your assignments to focus on the writer, the reality (topic, subject), or the reader (audience). Expressive writing focuses on the writer and her or his experience with the subject. Informative writing focuses on the subject in a way that the writer informs the reader about the subject. Persuasive writing focuses on the reader whom the writer attempts to convince to believe something or to act in a certain way. The sequencing involved here considers the difficulties of the tasks involved. Expressive writing is supposedly easier to produce than persuasive writing.

Regardless of what sequence you devise for your students' writing assignments, you will, on occasion, want to allow them some freedom to select whatever mode, objective, or type of writing they feel best meets the assignment. They need such experience to prepare them for writing that lies beyond your course both inside and outside of academia.

Directions and Due Dates

Because you have devoted a considerable amount of effort and time to designing your writing assignments, you will want to be certain that your students fully understand the expectation for each assignment. Instead of announcing the topic and your expectations for the assignment, provide these in writing; then read them together and explain them to the class.

The advantages of providing the directions in writing are rather self-evident: it should eliminate the ambiguities and misunderstandings that often occur when presenting directions orally. The directions appear in the instructor's prose, not that of the student; therefore, consulting them a day or two after receiving them gives the student a sense of confidence and alleviates much worry and misunderstanding. You can provide absentees with the written directions saving some of your time before or after classes.

Other advantages accrue to the instructor as well. As the semester progresses, you can easily consult your assignment topics and directions to review and ascertain that you are indeed following the sequence for assignments designed for your course to reinforce your philosophy of composition. If for some reason you have deviated from the sequence, you can readily determine when and where. Finally, if you note that a student has not met the requirements of the assignment, you have a copy of the directions to substantiate your claim.

Some instructors believe that students benefit more from frequent short writing assignments than infrequent long ones: ten essays of three-to-four-pages in length versus two ten-page essays. The rationale is that the more often a student can receive feedback from the instructor and/or peers on the writing, the more guidance he or she has in attempts to improve the writing. Other instructors favor the longer essay assignments as the only way for students to gain experience with larger bodies of material. These instructors, as a rule, teach the longer essays in the process approach and provide feedback as the paper evolves. The deciding factor on the frequency of writing assignments might well lie in the amount of intervention by the instructor or peers in the writing process.

You will want to list the due dates for essays, determined by you before the course begins, in your syllabus. Distribute and explain each essay assignment a minimum of seven days in advance of the due date, preferably ten days. To do so in less time will simply impede the composition process. You will do well to remind your students, constantly, of the process between the assignment and the due date: "Have you prewritten yet?" "How's your first draft progressing?" "Are you into your third draft yet?" "Have you really re-visioned as you revised?" "Save your proofreading until later: Consider revising one more time and producing another draft." "Remember to include format considerations when you proof and edit."

You might request that students place their essays on your desk in the classroom at the beginning of the session on the day they are due; otherwise, most students will not be attentive to the new business of the day and will busy themselves with proofreading. Or you may opt to devote the first five to ten minutes of the class to an exchange centered on proofing. You will need to formulate and announce a policy for the late submission of essays. Most instructors lower the essay's grade one full grade for each day that it is late unless, of course, the student provides an official or convincing excuse for the tardiness. Promptness is a part of the discipline of writing. Theoretically, a written product can be revised hundreds of times; however, a time comes when the process must be interrupted and the product submitted for evaluation. We live in a world of deadlines.

Suggested Topics for Writing Assignments

Some suggested topics for writing assignments appear earlier in this Guide (see Chapter 3 for suggested topics for diagnostic essays; Chapter 6 for a listing of related-sentence exercises, the subjects of which are suitable topics for writing as well as for twenty-one suggestions for journal writing; and Chapter 9 for sample topics based on cognitive objectives).

Some composition instructors select topics for student writing that relate directly to the reading materials for the course, as in a composition class that has an anthology-reader as one of the texts or in a writing-across-the-curriculum (WAC) course. Other composition instructors select topics that relate to the sequencing of writing assignments such as those based on the rhetorical modes, the expressive-informative-persuasive axis, the cognitive-affective outcomes, or combinations of these (see Chapter 9 in this Guide). Additionally, some teachers select topics for "on-the-spot" (usually timed) writings to heighten awareness of particular senses (as for descriptive writing), or particular aspects of a problem (e.g., the second of three reasons why a student selected a particular college), or a series of related topics as preparation for the next essay. Whether the writing topics, then, stem from reading, memory, research, concrete experience, or imagination, try to select topics for writing that enable the author to learn or to see something in a new or different manner; or, as in many WAC courses, to serve in lieu of in-class examinations.

Topics for "On-the-Spot" Writing or Paragraphs

<u>Sense Enhancement via Description</u>

TOUCH:	wet chewing gum	a rubber band	a wet tea bag
	transparent tape	a tree trunk	a rope
	a stone or rock	flower petals	a curb
	running water	magazine pages	a metal key
TASTE:	an apple	a steak	pasta
	a drink of water	potatoes	coffee
	Gatorade	toothpaste	soda
	chocolate	popcorn	a pencil eraser
SMELL:	newly mown grass	perspiration	old books
	cigarette smoke	dirty socks	baby powder
	coffee	lake water	garbage
	auto exhaust	popcorn	a rose

HEARING:	guitars	running water	thunder
	an air conditioner	an alarm clock	a crying child
	a siren	a barking dog	an airplane
	tearing paper	rainfall	traffic

SIGHT:	shoes	a price tag	a license plate
	a leaf	newspaper headlines	a boat
	a restaurant sign	a tee shirt	a lamp
	a paper clip	a tree or shrub	a book cover

REACTIONS

shopping in a college bookstore
the college library
the college cafeteria
the first day of classes
peer collaboration and/or editing
nonsexist use of language
smoking restrictions
first use of a computer
first airplane trip
the last World Series in baseball
holiday bowl games
witnessing an accident

The traditional rhetorical modes of discourse can be paradigmed under the categories of expressive/informative/persuasive, bearing in mind that some modes will fall into more than one category. For example, classification can represent expressive writing if the author focuses on a personal experience, as in "the types of music I enjoy the most." It can also represent informative writing if the author focuses on the subject, as in "the types of music;" or as persuasive writing if the author focuses on winning the agreement of the audience, as in "heavy metal is the more enjoyable of the types of rock music." The following suggestions for writing in the rhetorical modes can, then, be adapted to suit other sequences of writing. Remember, though, that seldom does an essay employ only one of the modes. Rather, the modes are best viewed as patterns of paragraph development, as presented in the Modern Writer's Handbook, the combinations of which result in an essay dominantly expressive, informative, or persuasive.

DESCRIPTION

a grandparent	a student election campaign
a painting or poster	a happy marriage
grocery shopping	a magazine
a pet animal	a pet peeve
jogging clothes	a favorite food

COMPARISON/CONTRAST

evening television programs   news via print/television

magazine ads for cigarettes
foreign and domestic cars
letters to an editor
high school/college English classes
convenience store/supermarket shopping

roles for men and women in society
women's and men's sports
two enjoyable movies
summer work experiences
live drama verses movie versions

CLASSIFICATION

mail advertisements
students in a dormitory
people at a bus stop
clothing for exercising
morning television programs
rock bands

pets
customers at a convenience store
consumers of alcoholic beverages
wearers of ball caps
weekly news magazines
foreign cars

PROCESS ANALYSIS

an aspect of a summer job
making a bow in a shoestring
writing an essay
serving a tennis ball
swimming a particular stroke
how to start an auto

an aspect of camping
grilling a steak
cleaning rain gutters
sewing something
preparing for a competition
getting a can of soda from a machine

DEFINITION

a happy family
a politician
a thing of beauty
a referee's responsibilities
a concept of patriotism
a concept of single parenthood

a good day-care center
a latch-key child
an impartial newspaper
a good teacher
an ineffective television commercial
a good movie

ANALYSIS

designing the interior of a car
college alcohol policies
discipline in study habits
a decision not to participate in X
what constitutes a failing essay
women in sports

restrictions on financial aid scholarships
a recent newspaper editorial
class attendance policies in college
the role of television in election campaigns
college dress codes or lack thereof
required subjects in college

ARGUMENT/PERSUASION

controlled cigarette smoking
national health insurance
student rights
single-sex dormitories
federal/state child-care centers

permission for teenage abortions
free public transportation
campus newspaper censorship
equal pay for equal work
free college tuition

benefits for disabled persons	required military service
effects of electromagnetic fields	urban garbage disposal
population controls	pesticide pollution
children suing parents	wealth is more than money
tax support for private schools	banning boxing as a sport
the value of grading systems	women in military combat

Works Cited

Bloom, Benjamin S., ed. <u>Taxonomy of Educational Objectives: The Classification of Educational Goals. Handbook 1 Cognitive Domain</u>. London: Longmans, 1956.

Booth, Wayne C. "Boring from Within: The Art of the Freshman Essay." Speech delivered May, 1963 to the Illinois Council of College Teachers of English.

Krathwohl, David R., Benjamin S. Bloom, and Bertran B. Masia. <u>Taxonomy of Educational Objectives: The Classification of Educational Goals. Handbook II Affective Domain</u>. London: David McKay Co., 1964.

Lindemann, Erika. <u>A Rhetoric for Writing Teachers</u>. 2nd ed. New York: Oxford UP, 1987.

Williams, James D. <u>Preparing to Teach Writing</u>. Belmont, CA: Wadsworth, 1989.

For Further Reading

New teachers can benefit by consulting Thomas A. Angelo and K. Patricia Cross, <u>Classroom Assessment Techniques: A Handbook for College Teachers</u>, 2nd ed. (San Francisco: Jossey-Bass, 1993) and Cheryl F. Fischer and Rita M. King, <u>Authentic Assessment: A Guide to Implementation</u> (San Francisco: Corvin, 1995). Also of interest are Bruce Lawson, et al., <u>Encountering Student Texts: Interpretive Issues in Reading Student Writing</u> (Urbana: National Council of Teachers of English, 1989); Robert J. Connors and Andrea A. Lunsford, "Teacher's Rhetorical Comments on Student Papers," (<u>College Composition and Communication</u> 44 [1993]: 200-23); Peter Elbow, "Ranking, Evaluating, Linking: Sorting Out Three Forms of Judgments," (<u>College English</u> 55 [1993]: 187-206); and Edward M. White, <u>Teaching and Assessing Writing</u>, 2nd ed. (San Francisco: Jossey-Bass, 1994).

CHAPTER 10. ASSESSING WRITING

It is helpful to instructors to think of writing assessment as two processes: formative and summative. The terms formative and summative evaluation were introduced by Michael Scriven in a 1967 AERA monograph. Formative evaluation consists of "assessment that takes place during the developmental (formative) stages of a program or a product." In contrast, summative evaluation consists of "assessment of the overall effectiveness of a program or a product." Formative evaluation of writing, then, helps students "move from first drafts to genuine revised drafts" (White 278). Instructors engage in formative evaluation when they confer with students on drafts, when they arrange for and encourage peer editing among student groups, when they comment on drafts with an eye toward revision. Summative evaluation of writing, in contrast, occurs at the completed draft stage. Instructors engage in summative evaluation when they evaluate the finished product and explain to the student the reasons for the grade assigned.

Before engaging in the modes, levels, and procedures of assessing student writing, most writing teachers benefit by reminding themselves to stress the concept that evaluation can be a teaching device and a part of the writing process. In discussing these evaluation activities, especially with students, it becomes important not to refer to them collectively as "correcting your writing." The connotation of this phrase sends a negative message to students. You, as a writing instructor, are evaluating or assessing a product that results from a process in terms of its completeness or lack of completeness; hence, the writing is not "right" or "wrong"; instead of this static dualism, the writing reflects varying stages of completeness or dynamism as the product evolves from the process. You will need to decide whether your evaluations will be summative, formative, or some combination of the two methods. If you want the writing process to be more than a mere academic exercise for students, consider adopting an evaluative procedure that combines the formative and summative assessment techniques.

Modes of Evaluation

You have a number of options from which to select an appropriate mode of evaluation: by written commentary, by individual conference, by peer critique, by oral commentary on audiotape, by portfolio commentary, by computer commentary, and by various combinations of these options.

Evaluation of student writing by **written commentary** constitutes the most widely used mode, but not all written commentary is helpful to students. The absence of written commentary sends a devastating message to the student ("Did my teacher even read the essay?") and is a negation of the skill and art you are teaching. To impart helpful order to your written commentaries, first adopt a systematic order for the writing you place on students' essays. You might reserve the interlinear spaces for recording only the revision symbols that are keyed to the Handbook. These symbols will help the student find the locations in the Handbook for appropriate advice. Reserve the paper's margins for your questions. Instead of marginalia that use the imperative mood ("Don't do this!") or a sarcastic tone ("Whatever that means!"), try using interrogatives ("Why this?" and "What does this mean?"). Such prompts will help lead your students to discover a response. You might suggest that students keep a listing of the interrogatives that appear in the margins as an aid for their revision of future writing.

At the end of the essay, provide a summary for the student, one that brings together all your correction symbols and questions in a paragraph that is written in complete sentences. Also note here whatever patterns evolved in the writing that need attention, but avoid trying to fix everything at once, especially in the earlier stages of the course. Rather than overwhelm the student with advice on each and every mark that you have made on the essay, select a few major points and comment upon these. You might suggest some possibilities and options, but remember not to rewrite the paper for the student. This serves no real purpose. The task of evaluation does not include your rewriting of students' essays; students really learn nothing about revising from such activities. Students benefit best when they do the revisions themselves. Finally, always try to include a positive comment about the essay somewhere in the summary paragraph (e.g., "a very neat presentation," "good development in the second paragraph," "impressive supporting material"). Words of encouragement from the writing teacher (such as "I know you'll improve"; "be patient: this takes practice"; "improvement is evident since your last essay") are worth the time it takes to write them.

Another option for evaluating writing is the one-on-one **individual conference**. Because this process is very time consuming, some teachers use it only once or twice in the course. But others make it a part of the process for each essay assignment. See Section 2d in this Guide for a detailed discussion of teacher-student conferences.

Peer critique, also a mode of evaluation, is best reserved for the invention, revision, and proofreading-editing stages of the writing process, where evaluation in terms of a summative grade is not the impetus. The majority of your students lack the knowledge and experience that enter into instructors' decisions about evaluating writing; hence, students should not be asked to assign definitive grades to their peer's writing. Although students very much enjoy, either in small groups or as a whole class, commenting on other students' essays and offering advice that is non-directive, facilitative, and centered on revision, they do not relish assigning grades or receiving them from their peers. However, students have proven themselves to be quite perceptive and honest in self-evaluations.

Oral commentary by the teacher on audiotape results in very helpful, albeit lengthy and detailed, assessments of student writing simply because we talk faster than we write. And because we talk so fast, you may find yourself spending more time than you realize when using oral commentary. A colleague successfully limits commentary by using an egg timer. Unlike the student-teacher conference that results in dialogue, however, the commentary on audiotape is a monologue that the student listens to as she or he reads the essay. Address the student by name and adopt a pleasant tone. Begin your commentary as you read the essay and record your reactions, questions, and advice. Remember to turn off the recorder when you are not speaking. Include a summary at the close of your commentary as you would when using written commentary. The logistics for this mode of evaluation require the student to submit a audiotape with each essay in an envelope. Most students resubmit the same tape by rewinding it to its beginning or to the place where your last commentary ended. You might consider using the learning resource center or its equivalent as the return station for the essays you have evaluated, thereby insuring that your students have convenient access to a tape recorder to listen to your commentary.

Portfolio commentary is usually done by a committee of evaluators who evaluate either the entire contents of a portfolio or only student designated portions of the portfolio at periodic times during or after the course. But you can also involve students in this process through self-evaluation. Ask the student to write a brief summary of the learning process that led to each essay or to selective essays designated by you or selected by the student.

Computer commentary is gaining popularity in those writing programs where students and instructors have ready access to computers. Students either bring their disks containing the writing assignment to the instructor or send it via electronic mail. Several software programs for assessing writing exist: for example, PROSE or DocuComp. Keep in mind, though, that evaluation does not involve rewriting the product for the student.

Finally, combinations of the various assessment modes can be used to advantage as well. Combining written commentary with oral commentary, for instance, will provide your students with a very full evaluation of their writing. A combination of peer critique followed by your written commentary and/or self-evaluation can be a valuable experience. Students will be relieved when they do not have to assign a summative grade. Whatever mode of evaluation you select, and whether it is formative or summative, remember that you want to assess students' writing in terms of both strengths and weaknesses. Students who need a lot of help in improving their writing benefit from your encouragement. Avoid alienating them by your method of assessment.

Levels of Evaluation

When you evaluate the product that results form the writing process, you may be tempted to conceptualize it only in terms of the process: prewriting, drafting, revising, editing. Or you may think of it in terms of the process and the parts that make it a whole: organization and ideas on the one hand and paragraphs, sentences, words, mechanics, format, and style on the other. We segment both the process and the product for the purposes of pedagogy, but at the time of assessment, we consider the product for what it is: not the sum of its parts alone but the sum of its parts plus the principle of organization and how it reflects the philosophy of composition adopted in the course. Therefore, to assign two grades to an essay, one for "content and ideas" and one for "everything else," or one for "process" and one for "product," sends a faulty message to students. Good content and ideas do not exist independent of good organization, diction, grammar, mechanics, format, and style: these latter properties, no matter how perfected they are, strike us as academic experiences if they lack good content. Likewise, good process does not exist independent of a good product. Each instructor will have to confront this point, which appears to many as a dilemma in the evaluation process. Whether or not you adopt a holistic approach, your students, if they are to benefit from your assessments of their writing, need to and are entitled to know exactly what contributes to or detracts from what you consider to be good writing. We are accountable to students for the grades we assign them and rightly so. Avoid treating good writing as an elusive Platonic ideal; discuss it with your students and, upon request, explain each and every grade you assign in detail. (See the NCTE guidelines for interpreting the holistic scale in Section 11c in this Guide.)

As a teacher of writing, you most likely are not insensitive to the amount of time and effort that goes into the writing process. If you are, your students will not hesitate to remind you about their concern. But writing teachers evaluate writing, not sweat and tears. You can remind students that some writers complete the process quicker than others and, relatively, with more ease. We have no way of verifying or assessing the time students report they devoted to the process when we evaluate an essay. The grade assigned to the writing represents the completeness or lack thereof for the process-product. This also, in turn, reflects the student author's priorities. Informing your students of this fact will not only make them aware of your position on this issue but will also help them to understand the meaning of the grade assigned to their essays.

Procedures of Evaluation

Timing

Insofar as possible, schedule due dates for essays at a time when you can evaluate and return them to students by the next class session, especially if you assign penalties for late submission of papers. To delay the return of assessed writing will interfere with the learning experience that you want your evaluations to be a part of. Few students learn much from commentary on an essay returned two or three weeks after it has been submitted, no matter how thorough the evaluation. The sooner the student receives the evaluated product, the more he or she can learn from it because it then remains a part of that particular writing process. In addition, insofar as possible, attempt to evaluate a set of essays during a time in which you expect a minimum of interruptions. Avoid evaluating half of the essays on one day and half on the next: your standards will undoubtedly waver.

Implements

Use a finely sharpened black lead pencil to write your commentary on students' essays. At least any comments, if intemperate, can be erased! Red pencil or red ink marks carry negative connotations, which originated early in our students' academic histories. Again, as instructors, we want to provide honest assessments while minimizing all feelings of alienation and hostility that these marks may activate in our students. If you opt to use oral commentary, have extra batteries and tapes available for your tape recorder. If you and your students have access to computers, consider using one of the software packages designed for assessment.

Sample Annotated Essay. Following is a sample annotated student essay. Note the use of questions in the margins and the references to the <u>Handbook</u> as interlinear glosses.

John M. Mikel

Professor T. Crew

English 100

7 September 1993

FRIENDSHIP

Can "friendship" define? Don't we define words, not concepts?

Friendship defines the need for people to unite. In some instances it is for dependence upon one another and in others it is the effort only to fill a gap in life.

Why only a two sentence intro.? Try combining this with the next ¶ and recast it to include a clear thesis.

Friendship is a very delicate subject when defining it. There are different types. One type is a friendship with a family member. While siblings are friends they are also of the same blood. This changes the entire aspect of their friendship. A friend is usually attached to another by some feeling of affection yet with siblings thee is more than that. There is family, something a member can not just totally up and leave.

Note your over dependence on forms of "to be." Why not substitute more lively verbs?

wasted subject slot: 8a

Then there are friendships with the opposite sex. Friends of this type usually become intimate and continue serious relationships.

Effective transition?

right word?

wss

Although many times these relationships break apart

because of new found partners, especially with teenagers, a *23b* *13b*

lot end up in marriage. This takes on a whole new meaning *36d*

since they're not only friends but lovers too.

We as human beings depend on many things *trans.? 5d*

throughout our lives. As youngsters we depended upon our *23b*

parents to always be there when we needed answers about

our bewildering environment. To be there when we needed *9*

comfort and love to ease our pain or something new and *27a*

interesting to relieve our boredom. When we felt hungry *Such as? Can you be specific?*

they would supply us with food, and shelter when darkness *13b* *27e*

fell. While time pressed forward our dependencies toward

our parents began to deminish. We started junior high and *sp*

school work became demanding. So we had to depend on

our teachers and counselors and administrators to get us *23b*

through. There seemed to be thousands of new faces that *&*

frightened us so we clinged to our cliques from elementary *23b*

school. Yet they weren't always around *36d* *23b*

Margin annotations:
awk. meaning?
16 i
what is this?
what else would we be?
Enumerate here? note the length of this ¶
Try combining these sentences
spacing, ¶1
How does this relate to friendship?
what is the topic sentence of this ¶?
format ¶1

97

28a *7e* *why the passive?*

because classes kept us apart, therefore we were forced to

make new friends. Some of these friends we still have

today and some just didn't last. Many of the friends we

and senior?

made in junior high and high school were very nice and we *tenses*

16 f-h *25*

liked them, but some seem as though they were just for our

9d

use. Such as when we wanted to throw a football around

8a *11a*

and there were only a couple of kids you knew of that

13b *nice verb choice!*

could. We would spark a friendship only by using them to

25

play ball. Even as a child the only reason we maintained a

steady relationship with those around us was because of

34 *36d*

ellipsis spacing just that. . . . they were around us. We couldn't go distant *why not? In what ways?*

37

places as a five year old to meet people we thought were

better for us. We did what we could with whom we were

placed with, whether it be fate or coincidence. That is

36 a

when a five year olds mind initially decides upon who

38 *7e* *by whom?*

reword? he/she does and does not like. Since the child is given a *why the passive?*

24a

few kids to begin his life time search for friendship, he sees

29a, 44, 9b

a variety of personalities. Some timid, some disobedient,

98

what?
specify.

and others who are humorous. Charismatic kids, large kids,

kids who lead, or kids like sheep. With this based upon his

own personality and who he thinks possesses the most

positive qualities will become his standards towards who he

would like to meet or begin a friendship with in the future.

Why these
fragments?
what will?

Did you
check
verbs?

Although these standards are mainly subliminal and

abstract, they are a foundation for a molding he will be

building for many years to come. Throughout the

construction of this molding there are bound to be changes

which, in the long run, only make it stronger.

Is this a new ¶?

why the
pronoun
shift?

Now we move on into high school in our mid-to late teens,

and along with our dependencies toward our schoolmates

we find we depend on material things as well. Things like

the newly released, top of the line stereo or television with

frag.

all the bells and whistles to sit in our room right next to our

cordless phone. Then we will discover our desires to begin

a relationship with a member of the opposite sex and to do

logic?

so (we'll need a car.) A fire engine red Ferrari Boxer to be

precise. This opens up an entirely new world of friendship

one can't date without a car?

34
. . .dating! In this process of making friends we discover

not only finding qualities we like but display what we think

not clear

why?

to be our good qualities. All of these people we see

throughout our lives, of those I've named a few, become

our friends. We hold a tremendous friendship with our

on an equal basis?

parents and our peers. The faculty we've known throughout

our schooling have become our friends. The girls we've

27d
met although dating might have ceased are still our friends.

Condense

is
So I'd have to describe friendship as something you attain

through trials and tribulations. During the tough times in

life and through the gleeful experiences, the people who

23
stay close by are friends and will receive warm friendship

fusion

themselves. Friendship is a two-way street there must be at

106

29a
least two people who have some things in common, they

should like people and should be very compatible with all

/ frag.

awk:
/ reword

new ¶ here?
Generality!
Exactness?
This reads like
a conclusion.
End here?

All of them?

one?
don't preach!

what does this mean?

colon?

100

different types of people. The couple should respect each

other because if they didn't they would not defend one

against what? another. They probably would not stick up for each other

23 b

while the one partner was absent. In a group a peer should

24a   sp
feel comfortable, he should have a since of belonging and

Did you proofread carefully? not be left sticking out like a soar thumb. Making friends   *spacing*

has a lot to do with chance. May times we do not choose

our friends. It is more like we dabble with many persons

10a
whether we know anything about them or not, sometimes   *cs*

even if we've previously heard bad things about them we

23
will still go out with them and see for our selves. I've made

29.a
many friends over the past eighteen years, some good

some bad, and I am yet to master the technique of judging a

25   *done*
book by it's cover.   So I will continue to do as I have and

Meaning? learn about the people I consider to be a part of. I'll try not

25
to go wrong although that's hard to do at this college.

John: Your essay reads as if it were an unrevised first draft. You touch upon several very interesting possibilities re friendship that could nicely lead to a developed essay. Try comparing or contrasting sibling friendship with high school friendships, i.e. delimit and formulate a clear thesis. maybe more brainstorming would help? In re-VISION, insert transitional words/phrases to link paragraphs. Also eliminate overdependence on forms of "to be." Proofread very carefully to eliminate fragments, spelling/typos. The seeds of a good essay are here; I think you can do better. Don't get discouraged.

Assigning the Grade.

Use whatever letter or number system your college has adopted when assigning grades to essays: at least most people involved have some idea of what the letters or number signify. Many instructors opt not to assign grades to essays, especially early in the course. Other instructors believe students have the right to know, from the very beginning, the reaction their writing elicits. Still other instructors devise personal, sometimes esoteric systems of grading as on a scale of 7 or 9 or 13. Even though the teacher may fully explain the rationale underlying such grading practices, these systems tend to confuse students and academic advisors alike. This, then, defeats the purpose of a grading system: to indicate clearly where a student's writing ranks in terms of completeness of the writing process, whether on a scale of values from 1 to 100 or from "F" to "A." The use of single or double plus or minus signs, as in B++, although perhaps not sanctioned by your college on final grade rosters, can somewhat compensate for a lack of refinement in some letter grade systems and send a clearer message to the student.

Guidelines for Evaluating and Grading Essays[1]

<u>The Superior or "A" Essay</u>

1. General ideas receive clear development and support with appropriate specifics such as examples, illustrations, facts, and other details.

2. Ideas indicate a mature level of thought as evidenced by originality, insight, and/or the ability to draw inferences and make analogies.

3. The thesis reflects a clear purpose that receives consistent development throughout the essay.

4. The essay exhibits clear organization with a logical flow of ideas, including a beginning, a middle, and an end, and incorporates effectively selected transitional words or phrases.

5. The introduction effectively introduces the main idea, stimulates interest, and establishes the tone and audience of the essay.

6. The middle section contains fully developed paragraphs that reflect appropriate choices of developmental patterns.

7. An appropriate conclusion closes the essay.

8. Sentence structure includes variety, emphasis, and logical relationships.

9. Word choices are accurate and effective.

---

[1] The author wishes to acknowledge the participation of students enrolled in a graduate seminar on the teaching of writing, 1977-78, at the University of Notre Dame in formulating these guidelines.

10. Grammatical, mechanical, and format errors are totally absent or rare.

11. The essay clearly reveals a sustained sense of audience.

The "superior" paper distinguishes itself from the "good" paper by a more assured prose style, more creativity in form and content, and more effective uses of writing strategies.

The Good or "B" Essay

1. General ideas receive support by the selection of appropriate examples, illustrations, facts, and other details.

2. Ideas indicate a mature level of thought and are consistently clear.

3. The thesis contains a clear purpose that receives consistent development.

4. The essay exhibits clear organization with a beginning, a middle, and an end and presents a logical flow of ideas with appropriate transitional words or phrases.

5. The introduction effectively introduces the main idea, stimulates interest, and establishes the tone and audience for the essay.

6. The middle section contains fully developed paragraphs that reflect the selection of appropriate developmental patterns.

7. An appropriate conclusion closes the essay.

8. A variety of sentence structures exists.

9. Word choice is accurate.

10. A sense of audience is present.

11. Very few grammatical, mechanical, or format errors are present.

The Satisfactory or "C" Essay.

1. General ideas are usually supported by specifics such as examples, illustrations, facts, and other details.

2. Ideas are usually clear.

3. The essay's organization reflects a logical flow of ideas, including a beginning, a middle, and an end.

4. A sense of purpose and a controlling idea are at least evident, even if not sustained.

5. Paragraphs receive appropriate and full development. Transitional words and phrases are present but not used appropriately.

6. A few fragments or fused sentences or comma splices may remain even though some evidence exists that revision and editing did occur.

7. A sense of audience is present.

8. A mere absence of grammatical, mechanical, or format errors does not earn a grade of "satisfactory."

The Unsatisfactory or "D" Essay

1. General ideas tend to be supported by specifics such as examples, illustrations, facts, and other details albeit not systematically.

2. Ideas are frequently unclear.

3. The essay's organization is inadequate; the introduction and/or conclusion are absent or fail to function properly.

4. The middle section contains undeveloped paragraphs and/or lacks patterns of appropriate development, while transitional words or phrases are inappropriate or absent.

5. A thesis, if present at all, lacks restriction and/or unity.

6. Little or no sentence variety is present.

7. No clear tone is established.

8. A sense of audience is lacking.

9. Evidence of careless revision and/or editing is present.

10. Several grammatical, mechanical, and format errors occur.

11. The essay can clearly benefit from the recursiveness of the writing process.

The Failing or "F" Essay

1. General ideas lack support from specific details.

2. Ideas are consistently unclear.

3. Organization is flawed; the introduction and/or conclusion are absent or do not function.

4. No thesis is stated, or, if so, it is not sustained.

5. Paragraphs lack full development and/or have inappropriate developmental patterns.

6. Transitional words and/or phrases do not appear.

7. Frequent errors in sentence structure appear: fragments, fusions, splices.

8. Frequent errors in standard and written English appear: misspellings; punctuation; usage; subject-verb agreement; pronoun-antecedent agreement; inappropriate shifts in tense, person, number, voice; mixed constructions.

9. The essay does not fulfill the requirements of the assignment. Simply handing in an essay does not guarantee its author a "satisfactory" grade.

10. Little or no evidence of the use of the writing process is present.

Evaluation in the Writing Process.

Submitting the essay for evaluation interrupts the writing process. The interruption may be temporary or permanent. Because any writing product can be revised and refined again and again, and because multiple revisions have hopefully already been made to the product before a student submits it, you will need to decide whether your evaluation of the product terminates with stasis in the process or contributes to the dynamism of it. Many teachers adopt the former stance, believing it is better to begin the process anew with a fresh topic. Others expect students to do a final revision in light of the teacher's evaluative commentary and to resubmit the product for a final summative evaluation. If you opt for the latter approach, consider withholding your assignment of a letter or number grade until the final evaluation occurs.

Works Cited

Scriven, Michael. "Formative Evaluation; Summative Evaluation." American Educators' Encyclopedia, Rev. ed., Edward L. Dejnozka and David E. Kapel, eds. New York: Greenwood Press, 1990.

White, Edward M. Teaching and Assessing Writing: Recent Advances in Understanding Evaluation, and Improving Student Performances. 2nd ed. San Francisco: Jossey-Bass, 1995.

For Further Reading

The seminal work on **Writing Assessment** is Edward White's Teaching and Assessing Writing, 2nd ed.,(San Francisco: Jossey-Bass, 1995). Another work that provides background on writing assessment is Charles R. Cooper and Lee Odell, Evaluating Writing: Describing, Measuring, Judging (Urbana, IL: NCTE, 1977). For a discussion of large-scale writing assessment, see Karen Greenberg, Harvey Wiener, and Richard Donovan, eds., Writing Assessment: Issues and Strategies (New York: Longman, 1986). To learn more about portfolio assessment, see Patricia Belanoff and Marcia Dixon, Portfolio Grading: Process and Product (Portsmouth, NH: Heineman, 1991). For a study that details methods of responding to student writing used by effectively by teachers, see Sarah Warshauer Freedman, Response to Student Writing (Urbana: NCTE, 1987).

PART IV. WRITING IN THE DISCIPLINES

The Modern Writer's Handbook, Fourth Edition, devotes *Part VIII* to writing in the disciplines. The student-centered content concerns writing in the humanities in general and about literature in particular (see Chapter 53 in the Handbook). Also in the Handbook, Chapter 54 contains advice for writing in the social, natural, and applied sciences; Chapter 52 contains sample research papers for writing assignments in classes on government (MLA documentation style) and psychology (APA documentation style); Chapter 55 concerns writing essay examinations in any discipline; and Chapter 56 covers writing in business. Although each academic discipline has its unique subject matter, vocabulary (jargon), and preferred types of writing, all disciplines benefit from a knowledge of the writing process.

Chapter 11. COMPOSITION AND OTHER SUBJECT MATTERS

At many colleges and universities, a composition course exists in and for itself, (i.e., considered independent of any particular discipline). Yet the writing assignments are not about metacomposition (theories of composition) but about practical and idealistic matters based on memory, emotion, feeling, fact, intellect, and so on. Some professors describe composition as a discipline that has no subject matter of its own to write about. Most instructors agree, however, that composition is a skill-and/or process-oriented discipline that can effectively combine with the subject matter of various academic disciplines.

The duality of composition and literature in one course, for example, has a long history in this country most likely because the overwhelming number of instructors of composition in the last fifty years or so have earned degrees in literature from departments of English. Until about twenty years ago, very few of these instructors received any formal training in the teaching of composition except in a few enlightened graduate departments of English. Left to their own resources, the instructors did what they knew best: taught composition using the textbooks available at the time, most of which based all writing assignments on literature. Almost everyone who has taught a composition and literature course will agree that the kinds of narrative, descriptive, expository, and argumentative writing discussed in composition textbooks do not, on a one-to-one ratio, lend themselves to writing about literature, for which instructors expect and demand writing of an analytic and interpretive nature. But adjustments and compromises could be and were made. Instructors, then, need to acknowledge that writing about literature (or any other discipline) is a special type of writing that may or may not incorporate all the aspects of the kinds of writing taught in a composition course. One aspect that it does incorporate, however, is the writing process.

The birth of the Writing Across the Curriculum (WAC) movement approximately fifteen to twenty years ago sprang from two main sources. The first was the recognition that students can and must produce good writing in all courses, not just in the composition course. The second was that it is the responsibility of all instructors, not just those of composition, to teach writing. Lending credence to the first recognition was testimony from students themselves who cited the "anything goes" attitude about writing, with notable exceptions, that existed in their noncomposition courses. Upon graduation, some students reported never having written an essay after completion of the first-year composition course. As dissatisfaction with students' composition skills spread throughout academe, blame centered on the first-year composition courses. But the instructors of these courses accurately reported that students attained a certain level of proficiency upon completing the composition course. If those skills were not to atrophy, they had to be reinforced and built upon in other courses. Students should not be expected to retain and build upon the writing skills if other courses lack the required writing assignments. Acknowledging that disciplines may expect a writing product that differs from those in a composition class, we can agree that the one common practice all disciplines share is the process that leads to that product. And thus the Writing Across the Curriculum movement began to spread across the country.

The major problem instructors face when combining composition with another discipline is determining the amount of class time to be devoted to each. Rarely does an even split of 50 percent composition and 50 percent subject-discipline result. The ratio tends to be more like 60/40 composition/discipline if the course is a first course in the college-level sequence of writing courses. In those WAC courses beyond the introductory writing course, the ratio can reverse to around 60/40 discipline/composition. A provision needs to exist in any program that combines composition with another discipline to adjust the expected ratios in favor of composition for those occasions when the skill levels of the students enrolled in a particular section are not as developed as had been anticipated.

When composition combines with any other discipline, such as literature in a first college-level writing course, the following guidelines for the composition segment of the course are offered as a minimum expectation (chapter numbers are keyed to the Fourth Edition of The Modern Writer's Handbook)

> Chapter 1 Preparation for Writing
>   2 The Process of Writing: First Draft

3 The Process of Writing: Revision

5 Writing Coherent Paragraphs

7 Thinking Critically and Writing Argumentst

8 Phrases, Clauses, and Types of Sentences

22 Variety and Emphasis

23 Appropriate Word Choice

24 Sexist and Other Biased Language

25 Exact Word Choice

26-41 Punctuation and Mechanics

What these guidelines suggest, then, is that formal instruction for **Part II, Grammar** and **Part III, Sentence Form,** in the Handbook does not occur in the WAC course. Yet you may certainly encounter students in your class who need assistance in these areas. If a majority of your students fall into this category, you can expand the guidelines to include these points, but doing so will inevitably take class time from the other discipline that is a part of the course. Explore, then, some alternate possibilities. Is free tutoring available on campus? Can the writing lab or the learning resource center assist students with these problems?

In addition to devising a list of minimal guidelines for the composition segment of your course, you will need to create guidelines for the discipline you are teaching, including in them the kinds of writing expected in that discipline. Thus, in humanities-oriented courses, the guidelines might include writing the book report as well as analytic and interpretive essays (see Chapter 53 in the Handbook). For disciplines in the various sciences, the guidelines might include field research reports, lab reports, and technical reports (see Chapter 54 in the Handbook). Most discipline-centered courses will also include the essay examination (see Chapter 55 of the Handbook) and some will include the research paper (see Part VII of the Handbook). Because no one-to-one fit exists per se between the narrative, descriptive, expository, and argumentative writing that composition textbooks stress and the writing expectations of a particular discipline, students will need explanations and assistance as the writing assignments in the WAC course move between these two poles. Obviously, analytic and interpretive reports about literature, for instance, incorporate techniques of analysis and other patterns of development as well as organizational strategies found in the Handbook (see Chapter 5); however, converting these into a content and format common to writing about literary topics requires, in almost all cases, formal instruction.

The following syllabus for a composition and literature course can serve as a model for the combination of any discipline with composition. Simply insert references to the discipline where references to "fiction," "poetry," or "drama" ("FPD") occur in the model. After the first essay in the course, the remaining essays have literature as their subject matter.

11a. Sample Syllabus for a Composition and Literature Course (Sixteen-Week)

TEXTS: <u>The Modern Writer's Handbook</u>, 4th ed. O'Hare, Frank, and Edward A. Kline, Allyn and Bacon. 1996. (<u>MWH</u>)
An Anthology of Literature: Fiction, Poetry, Drama (<u>FPD</u>).

ATTENDANCE POLICY:

GRADING POLICY:

COURSE OBJECTIVES:

PLAGIARISM: Using anyone's words or ideas without appropriate documentation constitutes plagiarism. Plagiarized essays receive no credit and result in <u>course</u> failure with notification to your advisor and Dean.

NOTE: The instructor reserves the right to adjust the order and times indicated on this syllabus to suit the needs of the class; however, notification of such adjustments will be made in advance of the appropriate date.

Week 1. **a.** Administrative matters. Course objectives. Read "To the Student," Chapters "Preparation for Writing" and Section 47f: **"Avoiding Plagiarism"** in <u>MWH</u>; fiction, pp. 3-39 in <u>FPD</u>.
b. Diagnostic essay due. Assign essay one (description). Discussion of plagiarism. Brainstorming and clustering. Read Chapter 2: "The Process of Writing: First Draft" in <u>MWH</u>.
c. Reflection on diagnostic essay. Peer collaboration on invention. Other methods of prewriting. Read Chapter 4: "Writing with a Computer" in <u>MWH</u> and fiction, pp. 40-74 in <u>FPD</u>.

Week 2. **a.** Thesis, purpose, audience, and tone. Read Chapter 3: "The Process of Writing: Revision" in <u>MWH</u>.
b. Discussion of fiction: subject, theme, and plot. Read Chapter 51a: "Writing about Literature"
c. Peer collaboration on first draft. Discussion of fiction: characterization. Read Chapter 5: "Writing Coherent Paragraphs" in <u>MWH</u>.

Week 3. **a.** Discussion of revision as re-seeing. Introductions and conclusions. Read fiction, pp. 75-122 in <u>FPD</u>.
b. Peer collaboration on revising first essay drafts. Read Part III: <u>Sentence Form</u> and 41: "Manuscript Form" in <u>MWH</u>.
c. Discussion of fiction: setting, point of view. Peer collaboration on editing essay drafts. Read Chapter 24: "Sexist and Other Biased Language" in <u>MWH</u>.

Week 4.   **a.** Essay one due (description). Reflection on essay one. Read Part IV: "Clear Sentences" in <u>MWH</u>; fiction, pp. 162-215 in <u>FPD</u>.
b. Discussion of fiction. Assign essay two (classification).
c. Discussion of fiction. Peer collaboration on first drafts.

Week 5.   **a.** Discussion of writing about literature. Reread Chapters 9: "Sentence Fragments" and 10: "Comma Splices and Fused Sentences" in <u>MWH</u>; fiction, pp. 216-327 in <u>FPD</u>.
b. Peer collaboration on revising essay drafts. Read Chapter 11: "Verb Forms" and Chapter 51b: "Sample Literary Analysis" in <u>MWH</u>.
c. Peer collaboration on editing essay draft. Discussion of fiction. Reread Chapter 12: "Subject-Verb Agreement" in <u>MWH</u>.

Week 6.   **a.** Essay two due (classification). Reflection on essay two. Assign essay three (comparison and contrast).
b. Discuss poetry: subject matter and theme. Read Chapters 13 and 14 on pronouns.
c. Peer collaboration on first drafts of essay. Discuss poetry. Read Chapters 15: "Adjectives and Adverbs," 18: "Sentence Completeness," and 48: "Documenting Sources--MLA Style" in <u>MWH</u>.

Week 7.   **a.** Sign up for conferences with instructor this week. Discuss documentation. Read poetry, pp. 696-728 in <u>FPD</u>.
b. Peer collaboration on editing essay drafts. Discuss poetry. Read Chapters 16: "Shifts and Mixed Constructions," and 33: "Quotation Marks" in <u>MWH</u>.
c. Essay three due. Reflection on essay three. Discuss poetry: verse forms and meter. Read Chapter 53: "Writing Essay Examinations" in <u>MWH</u>.

Week 8.   **a.** Assign essay four (process). Preparation for in-class mid-term essay examination on fiction. Read Chapter 16f-h: " Tense" in <u>MWH</u>.
b. Discuss poetry: figures, symbols, images. Read Chapter 23: "Appropriate Word Choice" in <u>MWH</u>.
c. In-class midterm essay examination. Read Chapter 25: "Exact Word Choice" in <u>MWH</u>.

Week 9.   **a.** Reflection on essay examination. Peer collaboration on revising essay drafts. Read poetry, pp. 729-68 in <u>FPD</u>.
b. Essay four due with a minimum of three documented sources. Reflection on essay four. Discuss poetry. Assign essay five (literary analysis). Read Chapter 27: "The Comma" in <u>MWH</u>.
c. Discuss poetry. Read poetry, pp. 769-804 in <u>FPD</u>.

Week 10.   **a.** Discuss poetry. Read Chapters 28, 29, 30, 31, and 32 on internal sentence punctuation; and poetry, pp. 769-804 in <u>FPD</u>.
b. Discuss poetry. Read Chapter 54: "Writing for Business" in <u>MWH</u>.
c. Peer collaboration on job application letter and resume. Discuss poetry. Read drama, pp. 579-665 in <u>FPD</u>.

Week 11.   **a.** Job application letter and resume due. Peer collaboration on editing essay drafts. Read Chapters 34: "Ellipsis Points" and 35: "Italics or Underlining" in <u>MWH</u>.
b. Essay five due. Reflection on essay five. Discussion of drama. Assign essay six (argument). Read Chapters 36: "The Apostrophe," 37: "The Hyphen," and 38: "The Slash."

c. Discussion of drama. Read Chapter 6a-d: "Critical Thinking" in <u>MWH</u>.

Week 12. a. Discussion of critical thinking. Read drama, pp. 331-47, in <u>FPD</u> and Chapter 6c: "Writing Arguments" in <u>MWH</u>.
b. Discussion of writing arguments. Read Chapter 44: "Capitalization" in <u>MWH</u>.
c. Peer collaboration on invention for argumentative essay. Discussion of drama.

Week 13. a. Peer collaboration on first drafts of essay. Discussion of drama.
b. Peer collaboration on revising first drafts of argumentative essay. Discussion of drama.
c. Peer collaboration on editing first drafts of argumentative essay. Discussion of drama.

Week 14. a. Argumentative essay due. Reflection on the essay. Read drama, pp. 448-578 in <u>FPD</u>.
b. Discussion of drama.
c. Discussion of drama. Assign final essay.

Week 15. a. Discussion of drama. Read poetry, pp. 805-37 in <u>FPD</u>.
b. Peer collaboration on revising first drafts of final essay. Discussion of poetry.
c. Discussion of poetry. Administer teacher-course evaluation instrument.

Week 16. a. Peer collaboration on editing drafts of final essay. Discussion of poetry. Review Chapter 53 in <u>MWH</u>.
b. Preparation for final examination. Discussion of poetry.
c. Final essay due. Summarization of course objectives. Final examination as scheduled.

Teaching and Assessing Writing by Noncomposition Faculty

Instructors who lack graduate training in English departments and who find themselves assigned to teach writing intensive and/or Writing Across the Curriculum courses most often react first with disbelief and denial and then with acceptance, albeit with varying degrees. Hopefully, such programs have some sort of orientation and/or training workshops designed specifically for such instructors. If your program does not have such workshops, agitate to get them started and seek assistance from your colleagues who do teach composition. A good place to start is the office of the program's director or chair. Meanwhile, this <u>Guide to Teaching Writing</u> provides much advice to help the neophyte instructor, and this chapter proceeds on the assumption that your particular writing intensive or WAC course is not the first college-level course in writing that your students have experienced.

One of the first things you will want to do is familiarize yourself with the writing process (see Part I in the <u>Handbook</u>) as well as the commentary on it in this <u>Guide</u> (see Chapters 1, 6, 7, and 8). Seek clarifications and advice from your colleagues who teach composition and/or the director/chair of your program. Once you understand what is meant by the writing process, you will agree that the process crosses disciplinary boundaries. Pay special attention to the features of collaborative writing and peer editing. What our various courses share in common, regardless of their disciplinary centers, is interchange among people, ideas, and words. And it is this interchange, as represented by collaboration, that we introduce into the classroom in the writing process.

Although the end products of writing in the various disciplines differ in genre (analytic, interpretive, reports, memos, and so on), one feature they share is the incorporation into the process of writing the techniques found in Chapter 5 of the Handbook: the organizational strategies and the patterns of development. As you explain to your students the nature of writing in your particular discipline, build on this common fund of knowledge; for example, the inductive and deductive reasoning processes proceed in the same manner whether the subject matter is electrical engineering, animal husbandry, or art history. And descriptive writing, whether in anthropology, microbiology, or architecture, shares in common an expectation of a point of view and the presentation of details in some directional order. Process as well as cause and effect analyses can be incorporated into many types of writing: essays that trace plot progressions in literature, lab reports in microbiology, patient care reports in nursing, and so on. In short, explain to your students how the expository patterns of development that they wrote in their composition course can serve them in the writing that is characteristic of your particular discipline.

Leaving the macro-level of organization and turning to the micro-level of sentence construction and word choice, similar principles operate in your discipline as in a composition class. Grammar, mechanics, and format expectations are other universals. You will need to reiterate to your students that the expectations for good writing remain the same in all disciplines, and that the process to achieve them is also the same. Then point out wherein lie the differences or the uniqueness about the writing in your discipline, even though it shares certain things in common with other kinds of writing. Most likely the primary differences can be categorized as those of tone, audience, and arrangement of the content.

Although you may lack formal training in the teaching of writing, you have written essays, if not a thesis and/or dissertation as well, in your major subject area. So you do know something about writing and, without doubt, more than your students do. In terms of pedagogy, you need to understand that a writing intensive or WAC course in your discipline does not simply mean assigning more writing than would occur in a nonintensive writing course. What it does mean is incorporating the writing process into your course: providing instruction about facets of writing, scheduling class time to discuss and working on problems students have with writing, and one-on-one conferencing with your students about their writing. You can use the sample syllabus in Chapter 11 in this Guide as a starting point for planning these aspects of your course.

In terms of designing and assigning particular writing assignments, the major differences between your course and a composition course will center on the content of the assignments, which, in turn, will reflect the subject matter of your discipline. Your students, then, will not only refine their writing skills but will also reveal what they know about a particular subject matter. The materials in Chapter 9 in this Guide, then, especially on the cognitive and affective domains, will prove to be equally relevant for your planning of a sequence of writing assignments for your course.

Many WAC instructors feel they need the most assistance in the area of assessing student writing. Remember to treat the writing process and product holistically. You might be tempted to bifurcate it and assign one grade for the paper's disciplinary content and another grade for its presentation (organization, tone, audience, grammar, mechanics, format, and so on). Resist. Good content does not exist independent of its presentation and vice versa. (See Section 10b in this Guide.)

When evaluating student writing, you may wish to use the correction symbols on the inside back cover of the Handbook. See Sections 10a and 10c in this Guide for additional practical advice on assessing writing. Many times you will notice that something is awry with a sentence--a dangling participle, for instance--but you do not know or cannot recall the name of the error. Rather than overlook the error, mark it awk (awkward construction) or use the interrogative mode: logic or meaning? You may wish to adopt the portfolio system in your class through which students build and maintain a file of the writings they produce throughout the course. You will have evaluated all of the writings; however, the students select a certain number (designated by you) of essays and revise them in light of both your comments and their own new insights as they reactivate the writing process. These revised essays then become the primary basis for the students' grade in the course.

Reproduced here, with permission, are the guidelines for holistic evaluation of writing issued by the National Council of Teachers of English (NCTE) as guides for judges in the Council's annual achievement awards in writing for secondary school students. The guide is equally applicable on the college level.

Guidelines for the Holistic Evaluation of Writing

The written selections should be judged holistically--that is, in terms of their total effect-- using the following general guidelines:

6 Potential in writing fully developed for the grade level, distinguishing characteristics that give the writing an identity of its own

5 Potential realized, showing competence with language and control in the development of the topic

4 Potential evident, but unevenness suggests that the writer is not yet in full command of the composing process

3 Potential partially indicated, but limited by shortcomings that call undue attention to themselves

2 Potential obscured by major flaws in the thought and development of the writing

1 Potential in writing undeveloped
[The numerals represent scores arranged here in a descending order.]

In order to help judges differentiate more clearly between good essays and poor ones, the following analysis is intended to represent strengths and weaknesses in terms of those factors that should enter into the judgment of a written composition. Judges are left to determine gradations of these qualities between 6 and 1.

CONTENT

Strengths: *Weaknesses:*

Independence of thought   Preponderance of obvious statements
Writer's engagement with topic   Writer uninvolved with topic
Fresh insights   Subject treated perfunctorily

PURPOSE/AUDIENCE/TONE

Strengths: *Weaknesses:*

Focus and intent clear and consistent   Purpose unclear or unrealized
Language and tone appropriate to   Tone inconsistent or uncontrolled
  purpose and audience

WORDS: CHOICE AND ARRANGEMENT

Strengths: *Weaknesses:*

Concern for expressiveness and clear   Limited vocabulary or misuse of
  communication   words
Apt choice of words   Indulgence in cliches
Readable, unambiguous sentences   Awkward or faulty sentences

ORGANIZATION AND DEVELOPMENT

Strengths: *Weaknesses:*

Logical progression, easy to follow	Little sense of direction or organizational pattern
Adequate support and elaboration	Few particulars or examples as support
Sense of completeness and closure	Fragmentary thoughts, lacking cohesion
Meaningful paragraphing	Intent of paragraphing unclear

STYLE

Strengths: *Weaknesses:*

Fluent, readable prose	Prose either effusive or cramped
Sentence structure treated flexibly	Unvaried sentence structure
Appropriate use of metaphor, analogy, parallelism, and similar rhetorical devices	General absence of rhetorical devices
Occasional willingness to be daring in thought or word; signs of inventiveness	Tendency to play it safe with words and ideas

TECHNICAL QUALITY: MECHANICS

Strengths:

Sustained point of view
Tenses used appropriately
Grammatical accuracy
Ability to punctuate for clarity and effect
Respect for manuscript conventions: spelling capitalization, hyphenation

Basic Elements of Style

The concept of *style* in writing often mystifies instructors in WAC courses. Style results from the choices of words we make and how we put them together for a particular audience for a particular occasion. Assign the "Glossary of Usage" in the Handbook as a starting point for helping students refine their writing style. Then bear in mind the following points about style both to share with your students and as a helpful aid when you evaluate their writing:

1. Verb Choices. Does the author rely too heavily on the "to be" verb forms? Does the author rely too heavily on "-ing" verb forms? Does the author employ the weak passive voice? (See Chapter 7e-f and Chapter 15 in the Handbook.)

2. Pronouns. Does the author overuse the personal pronouns? (See Chapter 7g as well as Chapters 13 and 14 in the Handbook.)

3. Adverbs. Does the author overuse adverbs? (See Sections 7i and Chapter 15 in the Handbook.)

4. Padding. Does the author overuse compound constructions such as noun and noun, adjective and adjective, verb and verb, and so on? (See Chapter 25 in the Handbook.)

5. Prepositional Phrases. Does the author write excessively long strings of prepositional phrases? (See Sections 7j and 8a in the Handbook.)

6. Generalities. Does the author's word choice reveal an unwarranted preference for the general and abstract word when a concrete and specific one would be more effective? (See Chapter 25 in the Handbook.)

7. Tone. Does the author establish a consistent tone? If shifts in tone occur, are they warranted? (See Section 2a in the Handbook.)

8. Hedging. Does the author fail to take a stand and, instead, overqualify most of the statements, hedge, "play it safe," avoid issues? (See Chapters 23, 24, and 25 in the Handbook.)

9. Sentimentality. Does the author assign an intellectual importance or emotional response to something that is in excess of what is warranted? (See Chapter 25 in the Handbook.)

In addition, consider the following general points when evaluating students' writing:

1. What, exactly, did you expect students to write for this particular assignment? (See Section 5c in the Handbook.)

2. Did the author select appropriate organizational strategies and/or developmental patterns for this particular subject matter? (See Sections 5b and 5c in the Handbook.)

3. Do the introduction, body, and conclusion of the essay accomplish their purposes? (See Section 3d in the Handbook.)

4. Do the individual paragraphs and the essay as a whole reveal a sense of unity, coherence, and emphasis? (See Section 5a in the Handbook.)

5. Does each paragraph have a topic sentence? (See Chapter 5a in the Handbook.)

6. Have the format expectations been met? (See Chapter 41 in the Handbook.)

When appending your written evaluative commentary after assessing the essay, remember to include comments on the writing per se, not just its disciplinary content. And do remember to add something complimentary in your commentary! (See also Chapter 10b and 10c in this Guide.)

For Further Reading

Several useful collections can help you begin your reading on **Writing in the Disciplines**. Art Young and Toby Fulwiler, eds., <u>Writing Across the Disciplines: Research Into Practice</u> (Upper Montclair, NJ: Boynton/Cook, 1986); Toby Fulwiler and Arthur W. Biddle, eds., <u>A Community of Voices: Reading and Writing in the Disciplines</u> (New York: Macmillan, 1992); Toby Fulwiler and Art Young, eds., <u>Language Connections: Writing and Reading Across the Curriculum</u> (Urbana: NCTE, 1982); Lea Masiello, <u>Write at the Start: A Guide to Using Writing in Freshman Seminars</u> (Columbia, SC: National Resource Center for the Freshman Year Experience, 1993); and Rebecca M. Howard and Sandra Jamieson, <u>The Bedford Guide to Teaching Writing in the Disciplines: An Instructor's Desk Reference</u> (New York: Bedford Books of St. Martin's P, 1995). To learn more about the organization and administration of Writing Across the Curriculum programs, start with Toby Fulwiler and Art Young, eds., <u>Programs that Work: Models and Methods for Writing Across the Curriculum</u> (Portsmouth, NH: Heinemann, Boynton/Cook, 1990); Susan H. McLeod, <u>Strengthening Programs for Writing Across the Curriculum</u> (San Francisco: Jossey-Bass, 1988); and Roger Sensenbaugh, "Studies on Effectiveness of Writing-across-the-Curriculum Programs" (<u>Compositin Chronicle</u> 5 [1992]: 8-9).

CHAPTER 12. TEACHING WRITING TO NON-NATIVE SPEAKERS OF ENGLISH

Not all non-native speakers of English have problems when writing in English. Among those who do, most encounter difficulties with grammar, mechanics, format, organization, tone, diction, and so on: problems that are shared by native speakers of English when they write. But non-native speakers of English also often have a unique set of problems in writing that stems from their linguistic backgrounds. Under the guise of accommodation, do not overlook these special problems. When one considers the difficult double task the non-native speaker encounters when writing in English--planning sequences of thought and writing about them in other than one's native language--we, as instructors, need to be both helpful and compassionate. As Kaplan points out:

> The English language and its related thought patterns have evolved out of the Anglo-Saxon cultural pattern. The expected sequence of thought in English is an essentially Platonic-Aristotelian sequence . . . shaped subsequently by Roman, Medieval European, and later Western thinkers. It is not better or worse than any other, but it is different." (211-12)

The difficulties with thought sequences in English become magnified for the many non-native speakers from the non-European tradition. However, Scarcella reminds us that exactness in written grammar is just as important for these non-native speakers as it is for native speakers. "While the literature suggests that grammar mistakes are a normal part of second language development, if we do not grade our students <u>down</u> on grammar, they may even decide that grammar is unimportant or, even worse, they have already acquired enough English to <u>get by</u> in school" (157). Obviously, product goals of spelling, usage, and diction are important but they can be mastered in the process approach to writing.

When the instructor notes the presence of the type of problems that identify a non-native speaker, he or she might begin by requesting a conference with the student. During this conference, ask several questions of the who, what, where, when, why, how, variety in an attempt to gauge the student's aural-oral proficiency with the language. Try to ascertain how much and what kinds of reading the student does and ask yourself how this reading relates to the required readings in your course. "Students from non-Western cultures," as Johnson reports, "often possess good English language skills, but are at a disadvantage when a reading assignment demands native-speaker awareness of myriad aspects of Western culture" (iv). Rivers and Temperley add that in order to become good writers, students must be widely read to help them learn to process information in English and to think in English "so that their writing acquires the rhythms and associations of the

English-language speaker" (312). During the conference also attempt to ascertain how much experience the student has had with expository writing in the native language. If the response is negative, the problems of writing in English will undoubtedly be magnified. "A lack of competence in writing in English results more from the lack of composing competence than from the lack of linguistic competence . . ." (Kroll 49). If the student has had experience with expository writing in the native language, you may be tempted to suggest that the student write the essay first in the native language and then "translate" it into English. After all, one reasons, the writing process is the same regardless of the language used. However, Kroll responds with a study that "suggests that using one's native language first and then translating it into English does not necessarily produce better texts" (123), while Rivers and Temperley openly admonish that all writing, including drafts and revisions, must be done in English (322). In your first conference with the student, then, seek to understand the particular problems for both reading and writing that reflect the student's background. Assign such students to peer response groups carefully, most often pairing them with native speakers.

Recognition of the non-native writer's problems and understanding them are but beginning steps for the instructor. Remember, also, that classroom practices in the United States tend to be less formal than what many non-native speakers are accustomed to, and this environment may prove surprising as well as perplexing to them. (Consulting a book like that of Swan and Smith's, which lists the most common English language problems that speakers of specific languages encounter, can prove helpful.) The instructor must attempt to help the student writer to understand the reasoning behind the problems in writing in English and their elimination. If a student has problems with omitting the definite or indefinite articles, for example, a reminder of which article precedes a word beginning with a consonant is not of much assistance. The student, instead, most likely will benefit from a lesson on the presence or absence of these articles with plural nouns, mass (noncount) nouns, abstract nouns, place names, and so on, as well as a discussion of the other noun determiners: demonstrative pronouns, possessive nouns and pronouns, and the quantifiers (some, each, every, most, many, and so on).

Among the most common problems non-native writers encounter are the following:

> adjectives and adverbs: word order placement
> adverb clauses
> American/British spellings
> auxiliary verbs
> conjunctive adverbs

coordinating conjunctions

idioms

indirect discourse

mixed constructions

passive voice constructions

prepositions and prepositional phrases

verbs: separable (particle verbs)

　　　subjunctive mood

　　　tenses

　　　verbals: as direct objects

　　　　　　as adjectives

In <u>The Modern Writer's Handbook</u> the following exercises are useful for non-native speakers of English in terms of grammar.

<u>Exercise</u>	<u>Content</u>
7-1	Parts of Sentences
7-2	Verbs and Complements
7-3	Pronouns
7-4	Pronouns
7-5	Verbals
8-1	Prepositional Phrases
9-1	Sentence Fragments
10-1	Run-on Sentences
10-2	Fragments and Run-ons
11-1	Verbs
12-1	Subject-Verb Agreement
13-1	Pronoun-Antecedent Agreement
13-2	Pronoun-Antecedent Agreement
14-1	Pronoun Case
14-2	Pronoun Case
15-1	Adjectives and Adverbs
16-1	Shifts
16-2	Verb Tense
17-1	Sentence Ambiguity
18-1	Comparisons
19-1	Types of Nouns
19-2	Noun Quantifiers
19-3	Placement of Modifiers
19-4	Verb Forms
19-5	Verb Forms
19-6	Verb Forms
20-1	Prepositional Phrases
20-2	Parallelism
21-1	Concise Diction
21-2	Phrases
22-1	Appositives
23-1	Slang

At the word level, students may require assistance with verbs and prepositions in particular. While the forms of <u>to be</u> probably will not be problematic except in the subjunctive, the use of <u>have</u> as an auxiliary verb may do so. Fries presents some helpful advice in this regard (170-74):

1. <u>have</u> + <u>to</u> + infinitive form to express necessity, obligation .

   Students <u>have to</u> write essays.

2. <u>have</u> + <u>to</u> + <u>have</u> (as a main verb)

   Students <u>have to have</u> pens.

3. Variations:

   a. They <u>have had to have</u> students pay for their pens.

   b. They <u>have had to have</u> students <u>have</u> their parents send money for the pens.

   c. They <u>have had to have</u> the students <u>have</u> the money for their pens sent by their parents.

Separable verbs (often called two-word or particle verbs) can often cause difficulties because of the prepositional component. A listing of the most common separable verbs follows (ellipsis indicates that the particle can be separated from the main verb by an direct object):

ask . . . out	go over	put . . . out
better off	grow up	put . . . together
break down	hand . . . in	put up with
burn up	hand in	quiet . . . down
call . . . off	hand . . . out	run across
call on	hand out	run out of
call . . . up	hand on	shut . . . off
clean . . . up	help . . . out	speak to
clean up	help out	speak up
come across	hooked on	stay up

count on	leave . . . out	take off
drop . . . off	leave out	take . . . out
drop off	look into	take . . . over
fill . . . up	look. . . over	talk . . . over
fill up	look over	think . . .over
get along	look . . . up	throw . . . out
get rid of	make . . . up	try . . . on
give . . . away	pick . . . up	try . . . out
give away	point . . . out	turn . . . on
give in	put . . . away	wake up
give . . . up	put . . . off	wear out
give up	put . . . on	wear upon

Understanding prepositions can be facilitated, as Fries suggests, by demonstrating the meanings of common troublesome prepositions by moving objects (such as an pen and notebook) on a desk (76):

<u>behind</u>	<u>in</u> (<u>inside</u>)	<u>roll off</u>
<u>in front of</u>	<u>beside</u>	<u>on top of</u>
<u>under</u>	<u>go around</u>	<u>beneath</u>

Beyond the level of the word, the next most common problem is likely to be the idiom, those fixed phrasal constructions that defy sensible semantic decoding on the literal level: "to catch a cold," "to rain cats and dogs," "to let the cat out of the bag." Such constructions are native to the spoken variety of English; as such, their use in written English causes the discourse to become colloquial. Idioms, native to most languages, are phrasal constructions whose meanings, as a whole, differ from the literal meanings of the constituent parts of the phrase. Native speakers have little or no difficulties with these phrases, having mastered their meanings and uses at an early age. Non-native speakers, on the other hand, are often mystified by English language idioms, most of which are not even recognized as idioms by native speakers. A listing of common idioms follows.

about to	eat one's words	look forward to
all along	every now and then	make it do
all of a sudden	fly off the handle	make oneself at home
be a die hard	get cold feet	make the most of
be all heart	get down to business	might as well
be all wet	get out of hand	not to mention
beat around the bush	get on with it	on pins and needles
be broad minded	get over it	out of the question

be broke	get with it	pay attention
be broken-hearted	give a buzz	put it in black and white
be cheap	goes without saying	say the least
be hard on	hang one's head	see about
be heartless	hang up	set a watch
be high strung	have a ball	set one's heart on
be narrow-minded	have a change of heart	short cut
be to blame	have a clear head	show promise
be touchy	have common sense	sight for sore eyes
be uptight	hit upon	stand a chance
be up to one's ears	hold one's own	step on it
brush up on	hurt someone's feelings	straight from the horse's mouth
by heart	in the dark	talk heart to heart
call to mind	jack-of-all-trades	take a dim view of
chip off the old block	just as soon	take after someone
close call	keep an eye on	tell it like it is
crack up	keep an eye out for	up in the clouds
do one's best	keep tabs on	wash one's hands of it
do without	keep your chin up	watch your step
down to earth	little by little	wet behind the ears
eager beaver	live from hand to mouth	

Unlike English, many non-Germanic languages lack prepositions, and some of your students will need assistance with prepositional phrases. First, be certain the student understands the concepts that the prepositions express: why we write "I rode to school on the bus" instead of "I rode to school in the bus." Check the list of common prepositions in the Handbook and ascertain that the student first understands their semantic dimension; then provide practice for the construction of prepositional phrases. At the same time, distinguish between the prepositions and the particle (separable) verbs: the differences between "up the stairs" and "to give up"/"to give it up."

On the level of the sentence, some practice in sentence combining (see Chapter 6 in the Handbook) will help the student with syntax problems, but recall that sentence contraction can also make written English "more concise and succinct if certain clauses are reduced to phrases (before he began the lecture → before beginning the lecture) . . . and some phrases reduced to single words (the man who drives the cab → the cab driver)" (Rivers and Temperley 303). As additional practice in composition techniques, Arapoff suggests the use of a simple dialogue as a base which the student rewrites in the forms of "direct address, narrative, paraphrase, summary, factual analysis, assertion, in essay form as argumentative analysis with evaluation of the argument, [and] as a critical review which objectively examines the validity of the evidence" (cited in Rivers and Temperley 314).

Some very practical applications can be found in Robinson's call for "controlled writing" practice; i.e. "writing in which a student cannot make a serious error if he [sic] follows directions" (265). A summary of her suggestions follows (265-70):

1. Turn questions into a statement as in "Is it raining?" "It is raining."

2. Turn two paragraphs of questions of the yes/no types into statements.

3. Respond to two paragraphs of either/or questions by writing statements.

4. Fill-in the blank space in paragraphs by putting although or until in each blank space.

5. Fill-in the blank spaces in paragraphs by supplying an adverb of frequency such as often, frequently, seldom, rarely, or never in each blank space.

6. Write a paragraph about X alternating sentences beginning with There and It.

7. Turn questions in the present perfect tense into statements in the present perfect tense and then the past tense.

8. Complete a series of "if clauses" by supplying would, could, might and a simple form of a verb.

9. Turn direct statements into indirect ones.

10. Supply a partial sentence to generate free writing.

Equal in variety and interest are suggestions for improving syntax provided by Frey, summarized as follows (65-78):

1. Change statements into questions that begin with "When," "Where," "How" "Why," "Who," or "What" and provide an answer:
The sun will shine tomorrow. When will the sun shine? Tomorrow.

2. To drill verbs, omit the -s and -ed suffixes and supply incorrect past tense and past participle forms, especially for irregular verbs.

3. Supply pronouns case drills of the nature:

he and I went   tell her and me

between you and me   wait for him and me

and, especially for speakers of Spanish, drills to correct this type of error: My sister lost his book; My brother lost her book.

4. For speakers of Asian languages, supply vocabulary drills with articles: an orange, an apple, a banana, a pear.

Contact your campus writing lab/ or resource learning center to discover the assistance available for non-native writers and encourage your students, as appropriate, to seek this help. The non-native speaker who has difficulties with writing English will face the same problems that native writers who write poorly will face when they leave your composition course. One should not, then, ignore the problem. Very few professors or employers will make special allowances for the non-native speaker with substandard written communication skills.

Works Cited

Croft, Kenneth. Readings on English as a Second Language for Teachers and Teacher Trainees. 2nd ed. Cambridge: Winthrop, 1980.

Fries, Charles C. "Have as a Function Word." Teaching English as a Second Language: A Book of Readings. Ed. Harold B. Allen. New York: McGraw-Hill. 1965.

Johnson, Judith Anne. Writing Strategies for ESL Students. New York: Macmillan, 1983.

Kaplan, Robert B. "Contrastive Rhetoric and the Teaching of Composition." Teachers of English to Speakers of Other Languages Quarterly 1 (1967): 10-16.

Kroll, Barbara, ed. Second Language Writing: Research Insights for the Classroom. Cambridge: Cambridge UP, 1990.

Rivers, Wilga M., and Mary S. Temperley. A Practical Guide to the Teaching of English as a Second or Foreign Language. New York: Oxford UP, 1978.

Scarcella, Robin. Teaching Language Minority Students in the Multicultural Classroom. Englewood Cliffs: Prentice, 1990.

Swan, Michael, and Bernard Smith, eds. Learner English: A Teacher's Guide to Interference and Other Problems. Cambridge: Cambridge UP, 1987.

For Further Reading

In addition to those works already cited for this chapter, some helpful books include Alice S. Horning, Teaching Writing as a Second Language (Carbondale: Southern Illinois UP, 1987), and Ilona Leki, Understanding ESL Writers: A Guide for Teachers (Portsmouth, NH: Boynton/Cook, 1992). The Leki, book is especially good at explaining what the research tells us about ESL writers and their language characteristics so that teachers can make informed judgments and hold realistic expectations for their ESL students' success. See also Scarcella, cited above, for sensitive and sympathetic advice to teachers who have language minority students in a multicultural classroom. See also Mary Ashworth, The First Step on the Longer Path: Becoming an ESL Teacher (Portsmouth, NH: Heinemann, 1992); Terry Dean, "Multicultural Classrooms;

Monocultural Teachers," (<u>College Composition and Communication</u> 40 [1989]: 23-37); and Pat Rigg and Virginia G. Allen, eds., <u>When They Don't All speak English: Integrating the ESL Student into the Regular Classroom</u> (Urbana, IL: National Council of Teachers of English, 1989).

PART V. SELECTED AND CATEGORIZED BIBLIOGRAPHIES

ENGLISH COMPOSITION JOURNALS

<u>ADE Bulletin</u>. New York: Association of Departments of English. 1964--.

<u>Advanced Composition Forum</u>. University of Nebraska-Lincoln: Association of Teachers of Advanced composition.

<u>Assessing Writing: A Bi-Annual Journal for Educators, Administrators, Researchers and All Writing Assessment Professionals</u>. Charlotte, NC: U of North Carolina at Charlotte, 1993--.

<u>The CEA Forum</u>. Lewisburg, Pa. The College English Association. 1970--.

<u>College Composition and Communication</u>. Urbana, IL: National Council of Teachers of English. 1950--.

<u>College English</u>. Urbana, IL: National Council of Teachers of English. 1939--.

<u>Composition Chronicle, Newsletter for Writing Teachers</u>. Livonia, New York: Viceroy Publications. 1987--.

<u>Composition Studies/Freshman English News</u>. Fort Worth, TX: Texas Christian University, (Formerly <u>Freshman English News</u>), 1993.

<u>Computer-Assisted Composition Journal</u>. Sanford, NC: Human Technology Interface, Ink 1987--.

<u>Computers and Composition</u>. Houghton, MI: Michigan Technological U and Colorado State U 1984--.

<u>English for Scientific Purposes: An International Journal</u>. New York: Pergamon Press. 1982--.

<u>English Journal</u>. Urbana, IL: National Council of Teachers of English. 1912--.

<u>Freshman English News</u>. Fort Worth, TX: Texas Christian U, 1972--.

<u>Issues in Writing</u>. Stevens Point, WI: University of Wisconsin-Stevens Point. 1988--.

<u>Journal of Advanced Composition</u>. Tampa: U of South Florida, Association of Teachers of Advanced Composition, and U of Utah. 1980--.

<u>Journal of Basic Writing</u>. New York: CUNY. 1978--.

<u>Journal of Business and Technical Communication</u>. Thousand Oaks, CA: Sage Publications. 1988--.

<u>Journal of Teaching Writing</u>. Indianapolis: Indiana Teachers of Writing and Indiana U/Purdue U-Indianapolis, 1981--.

<u>Notes from the National Testing Network in Writing</u>. New York: CUNY. 1982--.

<u>Philosophy and Rhetoric</u>. State College: Pennsylvania State UP. 1968--.

<u>PRE/TEXT</u>. Arlington: U of Texas. 1979--.

<u>Radical Teacher</u>. Cambridge, MA: PO Box 102. 1975--.

<u>Research in the Teaching of English</u>. Athens: U of Georgia, NCTE Committee on Research. 1967--.

<u>Rhetoric Review</u>. Dallas: Southern Methodist U. 1982--.

<u>Rhetoric Society Quarterly</u>. St. Cloud, MN: St. Cloud State U. 1968--.

<u>Rhetorica</u>. Berkeley: U of California P. 1983--.

<u>Teaching English in the Two-Year College</u>. Urbana, IL: NCTE. 1974--.

<u>Writing Across the Curriculum</u>. Odgen, UT: Weber State University. 1989--.

<u>The Writing Center Journal</u>. Logan, UT: National Writing Centers Association. 1980--.

<u>The Writing Instructor</u>. Los Angeles: U of Southern California. 1981--.

Writing Lab Newsletter. West Lafayette, IN: NCTE National Writing Centers Association 1976--.

Written Communication. Beverly Hills, CA: Sage. 1984--.

Writing on the Edge: A Journal About Writing and the Teaching of Writing. Davis, CA: University of California at Davis, 1989--.

WPA: Writing Program Administration. Logan, UT: Council of Writing Program Administrators. 1979--.

ASSESSMENT-EVALUATION OF STUDENT WRITING

Allen, Jo. "Approaches to Teaching: A Machiavellian Approach to Grading Writing Assignments." Technical Writing Teacher 15 (1988): 158-60.

Angelo, Thomas A., and K. Patricia Cross. Classroom Assessment Techniques: A Handbook for College Teachers. 2nd ed. San Francisco: Jossey-Bass, 1993.

Anson, Chris, ed. Writing And Response: Theory, Practice, and Research. Urbana: NCTE, 1989.

Arbur, Rosemarie. "The Student-Teacher Conference." College Composition and Communication 28 (1977): 338-42.

Bartholmae, David. "The Study of Error." College Composition and Communication 31 (1980): 253-69.

Bishop, Wendy, and Gay Lynn Crossley. "Not Only Assessment." Journal of Teaching Writing 12 (1992): 33-55.

Black, Laurel, Donald A. Daiker, Jeffrey Sommers, and Gail Stygall, eds. New Directions in Portfolio Assessment: Reflective Practice, Critical Theory, and Large-Scale Scoring. Portsmouth NH: Boynton/Cook, 1994.

Calpas, Gary, and William L. Smith. "The 'Expert Model' of Placement Testing." Composition Chronicle 8 (February, 1995): 4-6.

Connors, Robert J., and Andrea A. Lunsford. "Teachers' Rhetorical Comments on Student Papers." College Composition and Communication 44 (1993) 20-23.

Cooper, Charles R., and Lee Odell, eds. Evaluating Writing: Describing, Measuring, Judging. Urbana: NCTE, 1977.

Charney, David A. "The Validity of Using Holistic Scoring to Evaluate Writing: A Critical Overview." Research in the Teaching of English 18 (1984): 65-81.

Dragga, Sam. "The Effects of Praiseworthy Grading on Students and Teachers." Journal of Teaching Writing (1988): 41-50.

Elbow, Peter. "Ranking, Evaluating, and Linking: Sorting Out Three Forms of Judgment." College English 55 (1993): 187-206.

Faigley, Lester, et al. Assessing Writers' Knowledge and Processes of Composing. Norwood, NJ: Ablex, 1985.

Finn, Seth. "Measuring Effective Writing: Cloze Procedure and Anaphoric 'This.'" Written Communication 12 (1995): 240-66.

Fischer, Cheryl F., and Rita M. King. Authentic Assessment: A Guide to Implementation. San Francisco: Corwin, 1995.

Greenburg, Karen L. "Assessing Writing: Theory and Practice." New Directions for Teaching and Learning 34 (1988): 47-58a.

---, Harvey S. Wiener, and Richard A. Donovan, eds. Writing Assessment. New York: Longman, 1986.

Harp, Bill, ed. Assessment and Evaluation in Whole Language Programs. Norwood, MA: Christopher Gordon Publishers, 1991.

Haswell, Richard H. "Minimal Marking." College English 45 (1983): 600-04.

Haswel, Richard, and Susan Wyche-Smith. "Adventuring into Writing Assessment." College Composition and Communication 45 (1994): 220-36.

Huot, Brian. "Reliability, Validity, and Holistic Scoring: What We Know and What We Need to Know." College Composition and Communication 41 (1990): 201-13.

Kennedy, Mary Lynch. "Physician, Heal Thyself: Before You Assess Your Students, Assess Yourselves." Journal of Teaching Writing 12 (1992): 13-23.

Kroll, Barry M. and John C. Schafer. "Error Analysis and the Teaching of Composition." College Composition and Communication 29 (1978): 242-48.

Lawson, Bruce, Susan Sterr Ryan, and W. Ross Winterowd, eds. Encountering Student Texts: Interpretive Issues in Reading Student Writing. Urbana, IL: NCTE, 1989.

Lees, Elaine O. "Evaluating Student Writing." College Composition and Communication 30 (1979): 370-74.

Najimy, Norman C. ed. Measure for Measure: A Guidebook for Evaluating Students' Expository Writing. Urbana: NCTE, 1981.

Odell, Lee. "Defining and Assessing Competence in Writing." The Nature and Measure of Competency in English. Ed. Charles R. Cooper. Urbana: NCTE, 1981. 95-138.

Robertson, Michael. "Is Anybody Listening?" College Composition and Communication 37 (1986): 87-91.

Shaughnessey, Mina P. Errors and Expectations: A Guide for the Teacher of Basic Writing. New York: Oxford, 1977.

Sommers, Nancy "Responding to Student Writing." College Composition and Communication 33 (1982): 148-56.

White, Edward M. Teaching and Assessing Writing: Recent Advances in Understanding, Evaluation, and Improving Student Performance. 2nd ed., rvsd. San Francisco: Jossey-Bass, 1994.

Wiggins, Grant P. Assessing Student Performance: Exploring the Purpose and Limits of Testing. San Francisco: Jossey-Bass, 1994.

Williams, Joseph M. "The Phenomenology of Error." College Composition and Communication 32 (1981): 152-68

AUDIENCE

Ede, Lisa, and Andrea Lunsford. "Audience Addressed/Audience Invoked: The Role of Audience in Composition Theory and Pedagogy." College Composition and Communication 35 (1984): 155-71.

Elbow, Peter. "Closing My Eyes as I Speak: An Argument for Ignoring Audience." College English 49 (1987): 50-69.

Iser, Wolfgang. The Implied Reader. Baltimore: Johns Hopkins UP, 1974.

Kroll, Barry. "Writing for Readers: Three Perspectives on Audience." College Composition and Communication 35: 172-85.

Long, Russell C. "Writer-Audience Relationships: Analysis or Invention?" College Composition and Communication 31 (1980): 221-31.

Ong, Walter J., S. J. "The Writer's Audience Is Always a Fiction." PMLA 90 (1975): 9-21.

Park, Douglas B. "Analyzing Audiences." College Composition and Communication 37 (1986): 478-88.

COLLABORATIVE WRITING

Adler, Richard R. Writing Together, A Peer-Editing Approach to Composition. Dubuque: Kendal/Hunt, 1989.

Belanoff, Pat, and Peter Elbow. "Using Portfolios to Increase Collaboration and Community in a Writing Program." Writing Program Administration 9 (1986): 27-40.

Benesch, Sarah. Improving Peer Response: Collaboration Between Teachers and Students. ERIC, 1984. Ed 243 113.

Berkenkotter, Carol. "Student Writers and Their Sense of Authority Over Texts." College Composition and Communication 35 (1984): 312-19.

Bishop, Wendy. "Co-authoring Changes the Writing Classroom: Students Authorizing the Self, Authoring Together." Composition Studies 23 (1995) 54-62.

---. "Helping Peer Writing Groups Succeed." Teaching English in the Two-Year College 15 (1988): 120-25.

---. "Research, Theory, and Pedagogy of Peer Writing Groups: An Annotated Bibliography." 1986. ERIC ED 276-035.

Bouton, Clark, and Russell Y. Garth, eds. Learning in Groups. San Francisco: Jossey-Bass 1983.

Brown, Jane. "Helping Students Help Themselves: Peer Evaluation of Writing." Curriculum Review 23 (1984): 47-50.

Bruffee, Kenneth. "Collaborative Learning and the 'Conversation of Mankind.'" College English 46 (1984): 635-52.

---. Collaborative Learning: Higher Education, Interdependence, and the Authority of Knowledge. Baltimore: The Johns Hopkins UP, 1994.

---. A Short Course in Writing: Practical Rhetoric for Teaching Composition through Collaborative Learning. 3rd ed. Boston: Little, 1985.

Carter, Ronnie. By Itself Peer Group Revision Has No Power. ERIC, 1982 Ed 226 350.

Clark, Beverly Lyon. Talking about Writing. Ann Arbor: U of Michigan P, 1985.

Clifford, John. "Composing in Stages: The Effects of A Collaborative Pedagogy." Research in the Teaching of English 15 (1981): 37-53.

Crowhurst, Marion. "The Writing Workshop: An Experiment in Peer Response to Writing." Language Arts. 56 (1979): 752-62.

Cross, Geoffrey A. Collaboration and Conflict: A Contextual Exploration of Group Writing and Positive Emphasis. Cresskill, NJ: Hampton, 1994.

Ede, Lisa, and Andrea Lunsford. "Let Them Write--Together." English Quarterly 18 (1985): 119-27.

---, and Audrea Lunsford. "Why Write . . .Together?" Rhetoric Review 1 (1983): 150-57.

Elbow, Peter. Writing without Teachers. New York: Oxford, 1973.

---, and Pat Belanoff. Sharing and Responding. New York, Random, 1989.

Ervin, Elizabeth, and Dana L. Fox. "Collaboration as Political Action." Journal of Advanced Composition 14 (1994): 53-71.

Fey, Marion H. "Finding Voice through Computer Communication. A New Venue for Collaboration." See Computers and Composition.

Gaillet, Lynee Lewis. "An Historical Perspective on Collaborative Learning." Journal of Advanced Composition 14 (1994): 93-110.

Gebhardt, Richard. "Teamwork and Feedback: Broadening the Base of Collaborative Writing." College English 42 (1980): 69-74.

Gere, Anne Ruggles. Writing Groups: History, Theory, and Practice. Carbondale: Southern Illinois UP, 1987.

---. and Robert D. Abbott. "Talking About Writing: The Language of Writing Groups." Research in the Teaching of English 19 (1985): 362-81.

Gergits, Julia M., and James J. Schramer. "The Collaborative Classroom as a Site of Difference." Journal of Advanced Composition 14 (1994): 187-202.

Gillam, Alice, Susan Callaway, and Katherine Hennese Wikoff. "The Role of Authority and The Authority of Roles in Peer Writing Tutorials." Journal of Teaching Writing 12 (1994): 161-98.

Gilstrap, Tracy A. "Collaborative Computer-Assisted Composition Classrooms: The Solution to the Classical Problems." Computer-Assisted Composition Journal 5 (1991): 52-53.

Golub, Jeff, et al., eds., Focus on Collaborative Learning: Classroom Practices in Teaching English, 1988. Urbana: NCTE, 1988.

Goodburn, Amy, and Beth Ina. "Collaboration, Critical Pedagogy, and Struggles Over Difference." Journal of Advanced Composition 14 (1994): 149-166.

Grimm, Nancy. "Improving Students' Responses to Their Peers' Essays." College Composition and Communication 37 (1986): 91-94.

Guyer, Carolyn, Aurelie C. Seward, and Ann M. Green. "Collaboration and Conversation: Three Voices." Computers and Composition 11 (1994): 3-20.

Haring-Smith, Toni. Writing Together, Collaborative Learning in the Writing Classroom. New York: HarperCollins, 1994.

Harris, Muriel. "Collaboration Is Not Collaboration Is Not Collaboration: Writing Center Tutorials vs. Peer-Response Groups." College Composition and Communication 43 (1992): 369-83.

Hermann, Andrea. "Teaching Writing with Peer Response Groups." ERIC ED 307 616.

Holt, Mara. "The Value of Written Peer Criticism." College Composition and Communication 43 (1992): 384-92.

Huff, Roland, and Charles R. Kline, Jr. The Contemporary Writing Curriculum: Rehearsing, Composing, and Valuing. New York: Columbia UP, 1987 51-130.

Koschman, T. D. ed. "Computer Support for Collaborative Learning." See **Computers and Composition**.

Levenenz, Carrie Shively. "Peer Response in the Multicultural Composition Classroom: Dissenus--A Dream (Deferred)." Journal of Advanced Composition 14 (1994): 167-186.

LoNano, Mari. "Computerized Collaboration in Technical/Professional Composition." See **Writing Across the Curriculum.**

Lunsford, Andrea, and Lisa Ede. Singular Texts/Plural Authors: Perspectives on Collaborative Writing. Carbondale: Southern Illinois UP, 1990.

Mason, Edwin. Collaborative Learning. New York: Agathon, 1972.

Morgan, Meg. "Women as Emergent Leaders in Student Collaborative Writing Groups." See **Composition and Gender.**

Newkirk, Thomas. "Direction and Misdirection in Peer Response." College Composition and Communication 35 (1984): 301-11.

O'Donnell, Angela M., et al. "Cooperative Writing: Direct Effects and Transfer." Written Communication 2 (1985): 307-15.

Qualley, Donna J., and Elizabeth Chriseri Strater. "Collaboration as Reflexive Dialogue: A Knowing 'Deeper Than Reason'." Journal of Advanced Composition 14 (1994): 111-130.

Rabkin, Eric S., and Macklin Smith. Teaching Writing that Works: A Group Approach to Practical English. Ann Arbor: U of Michigan P, 1990.

Reagan, Sally B., Thomas Fox, and David Bleich, eds. Writing with New Directions in Collaborative Teaching, Learning, and Research. Ithaca, NY: State U of New York P, 1995.

Reither, James A., and Douglas Vipond. "Writing as Collaboration." College English 8 (1989): 855-67.

Roen, Duane H., and Geraldine McNenny. Collaboration As Plagiarism. See **Plagiarism.**

Smith, David. "Some Difficulties with Collaborative Learning." Journal of Advanced Composition 9 (1989): 45-57.

Smith, John B. Collective Intelligence in Computer-Based Collaboration. Hillsdale, NJ: Lawrence Erlbaum, 1994.

Spear, Karen. Sharing Writing: Peer Response Groups in English Classes. Portsmouth, NH: Boynton, 1988.

---, ed. Peer Response Groups in Action: Writing Together in Secondary Schools. Portsmouth, NH: Heinemann Boynton/Cook, 1993.

Stay, Byron L. "When Interests Collide: Collaboratin and Demolition." Composition Studies 23 (1995) 4-20.

Stewart, Donald. "Collaborative Learning and Composition: Boon or Bane?" <u>Rhetoric Review</u> 7 (1988): 58-85.

Taylor, Todd, and Joseph M. Moxley: "On Reviewing Electronic Discussions in Composition Studies." <u>The Computer-Assisted Composition Journal</u> 9 (1995) 18-21.

Trimbur, John. "Collaborative Learning and Teaching Writing." <u>Perspectives on Recent Research and Scholarship in Composition</u>. Ed. Ben W. McClellan and Timothy R. Donovan. New York: MLA, 1985. 87-104.

---. "Consensus and Difference in Collaborative Learning." <u>College English</u> 51 (1989): 602-16.

Van der Geest, Thea, and Tim Remmers. "The Computer as Means of Communication for Peer-Review Groups." See **Computers and Composition.**

Wiener, Harvey S. "Collaborative Learning in the Classroom: A Guide to Evaluation." <u>College English</u> (1986): 52-61.

Wyche-Smith, Susan. "Using Variables to Train and Maintain Writing Groups." <u>Composition Studies</u> 23 (1995) 63-77.

Ziv, Nina D. "Peer Groups in the Composition Class: A Case Study." 1983 ERIC ED: 229 799.

COMPOSITION AND GENDER

Atwood, Johanna. "Good Intentions, Dangerous Territory: Student Resistance in Feminist Writing Classes." <u>Journal of Teaching Writing</u> 12 (1994): 125-43.

Baron, Dennis E. <u>Grammar and Gender</u>. New Haven: Yale UP, 1986.

Bauer, Dale. "The Other 'F' Word: The Feminist in the Classroom." <u>College English</u> 52 (1990): 385-96.

Belenky, Mary Field, Blythe McVickcr Clinchy, Nancy Rule Goldberger, and Jill Mattuck Tarule. <u>Women's Ways of Knowing: The Development of Self, Voice, and Mind</u>. New York: Basic Books, 1986.

Bleich, David. "Genders of Writing." <u>Journal of Advanced Composition</u> 9 (1989): 10-25.

Brodkey, Linda. "On the Subjects of Class and Gender in 'The Literacy Letters.'" <u>College English</u> 51, (1989): 125-41.

Burnett, Rebecca E., and Helen Rothschild Ewald. "Rabbit Trails, Ephemera, and Other Stories: Feminist Methodology and Collaborative Research." <u>Journal of Advanced Composition</u> 14 (1994): 21-51.

Cain, Mary Ann. <u>Revisioning Writer's Talk: Gender and Culture in Acts of Composing</u>. Albany: State U of New York P, 1995.

Cameron, Deborah. <u>Feminism and Linguistic Theory</u>. London: Macmillan, 1985.

Caywood, Cynthia L., and Gillian R. Overing, eds. <u>Teaching Writing: Pedagogy, Gender, and Equity</u>. Albany: State U of New York P, 1987.

Crawford, Mary. <u>Talking Difference: On Gender and Language</u>. Thousand Oaks, CA: Sage, 1995.

Dixon, Kathleen. "Gendering the 'Personal'." <u>College Composition and Communication</u> 46 (1995): 255-75.

Flynn, Elizabeth A. "Composing as a Woman." <u>College Composition and Communication</u> 39 (1988): 423-35.

---. "Review: Feminist Theories/ Feminist Composition." <u>College English</u> 57 (1995): 201-12.

Frank, Francine Waltman, et al. <u>Language, Gender, and Professional Writing: Theoretical Approaches and Guidelines for Nonsexist Usage</u>. New York: MLA, 1989.

Gilligan, Carol. <u>In a Different Voice: Psychological Development and Women's Development</u>. Cambridge: Harvard UP, 1982.

Haswell, Janis, and Richard H. Haswell. "Gendership and the Miswriting of Students." College Composition and Communication 46 (1995): 223-54.

Hiatt, Mary P. "The Feminine Style: Theory and Fact." College Composition and Communication 29 (1978): 22-26.

Hill, Annette Olin. Mother Tongue, Father Time: A Generation of Linguistic Revolt. Bloomington: Indiana UP, 1986.

Kramarae, Cheris. Women and Men Speaking. Rowley: Newbury House, 1981.

Lauer, Janice M. "The Feminization of Rhetoric and Composition Studies?" Rhetoric Review 13 (1995): 276-286.

Lunsford, Andrea A., and Lisa S. Ede. "Rhetoric in a New Key: Women and Collaboration." Rhetoric Review 8 (1990): 234-41.

Miller, Casey, and Kate Swift. The Handbook of Non-Sexist Writing. 2nd ed. New York: Harper, 1988.

Morgan, Meg. "Women as Emergent Leaders in Student Collaborative Groups." Journal of Advanced Composition 14 (1994): 203-219.

Mullin, Joan A. "Feminist Theory, Feminist Pedagogy: The Gap Between What We Say and What We Do." Composition Studies 22 (1994): 14-24.

Takayoshi, Pamela. "Building New Networks From the Old: Women's Experiences With Electronic Communications." Computers and Composition. 11 (1994): 21-35.

Tannen, Deborah. Gender and Discourse. New York: Oxford UP, 1995.

Vardell, Sylvia M. "'I'm No Lady Astronaut': Nonsexist Language for Tomorrow." 1985 ERIC ED 266 472.

Zuber, Sharon, and Ann M. Reed. "The Politics of Grammar Handbooks: Generic He and Singular They." College English 55 (1993): 515-30.

COMPOSITION AND LITERATURE

Atkins, C. Douglas, and Michael L. Johnson, eds. Writing and Reading Differently: Deconstruction and the Teaching of Composition and Literature. Lawrence: UP of Kansas, 1985.

Biddle, Arthur W., and Toby Fuwiler, eds. Reading, Writing, and the Study of Literature. New York: Random, 1989.

Carino, Peter. "Alternatives to the Critical Paper: Teaching Against the Text in the Introductory Literature Class." Journal of Teaching Writing 12 (1994): 247-62.

Clifford, John, ed. The Experience of Reading: Louise Rosenblatt and Reader-Response Theory. Portsmouth, NH: Boynton/Cook, 1991.

Commeyras, Michelle. "Using Literature to Teach Critical Thinking." Journal of Reading 32 (1989): 703-707.

Delany, Paul, and George P. Landow, eds. Hypermedia and Literary Studies. Cambridge: MIT P, 1991.

Gamer, Michael. "Fictionalizing the Disciplines: Literature and the Boundaries of Knowledge." College English 57 (1995): 281-86.

Gould, Christopher. "Literature in the Basic Writing Course: A Bibliographic Survey." College English 49 (1987): 558-74.

Holman, C. Hugh, and William Harmon. A Handbook to Literature. 5th ed. New York: Macmillan, 1986.

Horner, Winifred Bryan, ed. Composition and Literature: Bridging the Gap. Chicago, U of Chicago P, 1983.

Lentriccia, Frank, and Thomas McLaughlin, eds. Critical Terms for Literary Study. Chicago: U of Chicago P, 1990.

Lindemann, Erika. "Freshman Composition: No Place for Literature." College English 55 (1993): 311-16.

---. "Three Views of English 101." College English 57 (1995): 287-302.

Lynn, Steven. "A Passage into Critical Theory." College English 52 (1990): 258-71.

Maimon, Elaine P. "Maps and Genre: Exploring Connections in the Arts and Sciences." Composition and Literature: Bridging the Gap. Ed. Winifred Bryan Horner. Chicago: U of Chicago P, 1983. 110-25.

Newell, George E. "The Effects of Written Between-Draft Responses on Students' Writing and Reasoning About Literature. Written Communication 11 (1994): 311-47.

O'Brien, Sheila Ruzycki. "The Medium Facilitates the Messages: Electronic Discourse and Literature Class Dynamics." Computers and Composition 11 (1994): 79-86.

Reilly, Jill M., et al. "The Effects of Prewriting on Literary Interpretation." 1986. ERIC ED 276-058.

Scholes, Robert. Textual Power: Literary Theory and the Teaching of English. New Haven: Yale UP, 1985.

Steinberg, Erwin R. "Imaginative Literature in Composition Classrooms?" College English 57 (1995): 266-280.

Swope, John W., and Edgar H. Thompson. "Three R's for Critical Thinking about Literature: Reading, 'Riting, and Responding." 1986. ERIC ED 273 985.

Tate, Gary. "A Place for Literature in Freshman Composition." College English 55 (1993): 317-21.

---. "Notes on the Dying of a Conversation." College English 57 (1995): 303-09.

Wentworth, Michael. "Writing in the Literature Class." Journal of Teaching Writing 6 (1987): 155-62.

COMPOSITION THEORY AND RESEARCH

Arrington, Phillip. "Reflections on the Expository Principle." College English 54 (1992): 314-32.

Beach, Richard, and Lillian S. Bridwell, eds. New Directions in Composition Research. New York: Guilford, 1984.

Berlin, James A. "Contemporary Composition: The Major Pedagogical Theories." College English 44 (1982): 765-72.

Bernard-Donals, Michael. "Mikhail Bakhtin: Between Phenomenology and Marxism." College English 56 (1994): 170-88.

Berthoff, Ann E. Forming, Thinking, Writing. 2nd ed. Portsmouth: Heinemann, Boynton/Cook, 1988.

---. The Making of Meaning. Upper Montclair: Boynton/Cook, 1981.

---. Reclaiming the Imagination: Philosophical Perspectives for Writers and Teachers of Writing. Upper Montclair: Boynton /Cook, 1984.

---. "Rhetoric as Hermeneutic." College Composition and Communication 42 (1991): 279-87.

Bizzell, Patricia, and Bruce Herzberg, eds. The Rhetorical Tradition: Readings from Classical Times to the Present. Boston: St. Martin's, 1990.

Booth, Wayne C. "The Rhetorical Stance." College Composition and Communication 14 (1963): 139-45.

Brent, Doug. "Rogerian Rhetoric: A Means for Changing Attitudes to Argument." Composition Chronicle 7 (1994): 6-7.

Carter, Duncan. "Critical Thinking for Writers: Transferable Skills or Discipline-Specific Strategies." Composition Studies 21 (1993): 86-93.

Charney, Davida, John H. Newman, and Mike Palmquist. "'I'm Just No good at Writing' Epistomological Style and Attitudes Toward Writing." Written Communication 12 (1995): 298-329.

Clifford, John, and John Schilb. Writing Theory and Critical Theory. New York: Modern Language Association, 1994.

Cooper, Charles R., and Lee Odell, eds. Research on Composing: Points of Departure. Urbana: NCTE, 1978.

Crowley, Sharon. <u>Ancient Rhetorics for Contemporary Students</u>. New York: Macmillan, 1994.

Crusius, Timothy W. <u>Discourse: A Critique and Synthesis of Major Theories</u>. New York: Modern Language Association, 1989.

D'Angelo, Frank. <u>A Conceptual Theory of Rhetoric</u>. Cambridge: Winthrop, 1975.

Emig, Janet. <u>The Composing Processes of Twelfth Graders</u>. Urbana: NCTE, 1971.

Fleischer, Cathy. <u>Composing Teacher-Research: A Prosaic History</u>. Albany: State U of New York P, 1995.

Flower, Linda S., and J. R. Hayes. "A Cognitive Process Theory of Writing." <u>College Composition and Communication</u> 32 (1981): 365-87.

---. "The Cognition of Discovery: Defining a Rhetorical Problem." <u>College Composition and Communication</u> 31 (1980): 21-32.

Foster, David. "What Are We Talking About When We Talk About Composition?" <u>Journal of Advanced Composition</u> 8 (1988): 30-40.

Fulkerson, Richard. "Composition Theory in the Eighties: Axiological Consensus and Paradigmatic Diversity." <u>College Composition and Communication</u> 41 (1990): 409-29.

---. "Four Philosophies of Composition." <u>College Composition and Communication</u>. 30 (1979): 343-48.

Gadamer, Hans-George. "The Expressive Power of Language: On the Function of Rhetoric for Knowledge." Trans. Bruce Krajewski. <u>PMLA</u> 107 (1992): 345-52.

Gere, Anne Ruggles. <u>Writing Groups: History, Theory, and Implications</u>. Carbondale: Southern Illinois UP, 1987.

---, ed. <u>Into the Field: Sites of Composition Studies</u>. New York: MLA, 1993.

Gradin, S.L. "A Writing Teacher Asks Some Questions Concerning Discourse Forms and the Culturally Diverse Classroom." <u>The CEA Critic</u> 56 (1994): 73-84.

Harkin, Patricia, and John Schilb, eds. <u>Contending with Words: Composition and Rhetoric in a Postmodern Age</u>. New York. Modern Language Association, 1991.

Harris, Jeanette. <u>Expressive Discourse</u>. Dallas: Southern Methodist UP, 1990.

Hairston, Maxine. "Different Products, Different Processes: A Theory about Writing." <u>College Composition and Communication</u> 37 (1986): 442-52.

Harris, Jeanette. <u>Expressive Discourse</u>. Dallas: Southern Methodist UP, 1990.

Hassett, Michael. "Sophisticated Burke: Kenneth Burke as a Neosophistic Rhetorician." <u>Rhetoric Review</u> 13 (1995): 371-390.

Hayes, John R., and Linda S. Flower. "Writing Research and the Writer." <u>American Psychologist</u> 41 (1986): 106-13.

Hillocks, George, Jr. <u>Research on Written Composition</u>. Urbana: NCTE, 1986.

Hunter, Susan, and Ray Wallace, eds. <u>The Place of Grammar in Writing Instruction, Past, Present, Future</u> Portsmouth, NH: Boynton/Cook, 1995.

Jarratt, Susan C. <u>Rereading the Sophists: Classical Rhetoric Refigured</u>. Carbondale: Southern Illinois UP, 1991.

Kinneavy, James L. <u>A Theory of Discourse</u>. New York: Norton, 1980.

---. "Theory, Theories, or Lack of Theory." <u>Composition Chronicle</u> 5 (1992): 5-6.

LeFevre, Karen Burke. <u>Invention as a Social Act</u>. Carbondale: Southern Illinois UP, 1987.

Moran, Michael G., and Ronald F. Lunsford, eds. <u>Research in Composition and Rhetoric: A Bibliographic Sourcebook</u>. Westport, CN: Greenwood, 1984.

Mullin, Joan A., and Ray Wallace, eds. <u>Intersections: Theory-Practice in the Writing Center</u>. Urbana: NCTE, 1994.

Myerson, George. <u>Rhetoric, Reason, and Society</u>. Thousand Oaks, CA: Sage, 1995.

Nelson, Cary, ed. <u>Theory in the Classroom</u>. Urbana: U of Illinois P, 1986.

North, Stephen M. <u>The Making of Knowledge in Composition, Portrait of an Emerging Field</u>. Upper Montclair: Boynton/Cook, 1987.

Nystrand, Martin, ed. What Writers Know: The Language, Process, and Structure of Written Discourse. New York: Academic P, 1982.

---, Stuart Greene, and Jeffrey Wiemelt. "Where Did Composition Studies Come From? An Intellectual History." Written Communication 10 (1993) 267-333.

Odell, Lee, and Dixie Goswaine, eds. Writing in Nonacademic Settings. New York: Guilford, 1985.

Olson, Gary A. "Rhetoric, Cultural Studies, and the Future of Critical Theory: A Conversation with J. Hillis Miller." Journal of Advanced Composition 14 (1994): 317-45.

---, and Sidney I. Dobrin, eds. Composition Theory for the Postmodern Classroom. Albany: State U of New York P, 1994.

Pemberton, Michael A. "Modeling Theory and Composing Process Models." College Composition and Communication 44 (1993): 40-58.

Perl, Sondra. "Understanding Composing." College Composition and Communication 31 (1980): 363-69.

Phelps, Louise Weatherbee. "Practical Wisdom and the Geography of Knowledge in Composition." College English 53 (1991): 863-85.

---. "A Constrained Vision of the Writing Classroom." Profession 93 (1993): 46-54.

Porter, James. Audience and Rhetoric. Englewood Cliffs, NJ: Prentice, 1992.

Pullman, George L. "Rhetoric and Hermeneutics: Composition Invention, and Literature." Journal of Advanced Composition 14 (1994): 367-87.

Ray, Ruth E. The Practice of Theory: Teacher Research in Composition. Urbana: NCTE, 1993.

Reither, James A. "Writing and Knowing: Toward Redefining the Writing Process." College English 6 (1985): 620-28.

Roy, Alice. "The Grammar and Rhetoric of Inclusion." College English 47 (1995): 182-195.

Scott, Patrick, and Bruce Castner. "Reference Sources for Composition Research: A Practical Survey." College English 45 (1983): 756-58.

Sommers, Nancy I. "The Need for Theory in Composition Research." College Composition and Composition 30 (1979): 46-49.

Summerfield, Judith, and Goeffrey Summerfield. Texts and Contexts: A Contribution to the Theory and Practice of Teaching Composition. New York: Random, 1986.

Tate, Gary, ed. Teaching Composition: Twelve Bibliographical Essays. Rev. and enl. ed. Fort Worth: Texas Christian UP, 1987.

Veeder, Rex. "History and Expressive Composition: Connecting with the Rhetorical Tradition." Composition Chronicle 7 (1994): 6-8.

Voss, Ralph. "Reassessment of Janet Emig's Composing Processes of Twelfth Graders." College Composition and Communication 34 (1983): 278-83.

Walzer, Arthur F., and Alan Gross. "Positivists, Post-Modernists, Aristotelians, and the Challenger." College English 56 (1994): 420-33.

Winterowd, W. Ross. Contemporary Rhetoric, A Conceptual Background with Readings. New York: Harcourt, 1975.

Young, R. E., et al. Rhetoric: Discovery and Change. New York: Harcourt, 1970.

COMPUTERS AND COMPOSITION

Anderson, Wallis May. "Computerized Invention for Composing: An Update and Review." Computers and Composition 9 (1991): 25-38.

Angell, David, and Brent Heslop. The Elements of E-Mail Style: Communicating Effectively via Electronic Mail. Reading, MA: Addison-Wesley, 1994.

Bean, John C. "Computerized Word Processing as an Aid to Revision." College Composition and Communication 34 (1983): 146-48.

Bolter, Jay David. <u>Writing Space: The Computer, Hypertext, and the History of Writing</u>. Hillsdale, NJ: Erlbaum, 1991.

Bruce, Betram C., Andee Rubin, Carol Barnhardt, and Teachers using QUILL in Alaska. <u>Electronic Quills: A Situated Evaluation of Using Computers for Writing in Classrooms</u>. Hillsdale, NJ: Erbaum, 1993.

Collier, Richard M. "The Word Processor and Revision Strategies." <u>College Composition and Communication</u> 34 (1983): 149-55.

Collins, James L., and Elizabeth A. Sommers, eds. <u>Writing On-Line: Using Computers in the Teaching of Writing</u>. Upper Montclair: Boynton, 1985.

Crew, Louie. "The Style-Checker as Tonic, Not Tranquilizer." <u>Journal of Advanced Composition</u> 8 (1988): 66-70.

Daiute, Colette. "The Computer as Stylus and Audience." <u>College Composition and Communication</u> 34 (1983): 134-45.

Dierckins, Tony. "Macintosh vs. IBM in Composition Instruction: Does a Significant Difference Exist?" <u>Computers and Composition</u> 11 (1994): 151-164.

Dornsife, Robert S. "Conversion of the Reluctant: Introducing Faculty to Computer Classrooms." <u>The Computer-Assisted Composition Journal</u> 8 (1994): 38-40.

Eldred, Janet Carey, and Gail E. Hawisher. "Researching Electronic Networks." <u>Written Communication</u> 12 (1995): 330-59.

Feldman, Paula R., and Buford Norman. <u>The Wordworthy Computer: Classroom and Research Applications in Language and Literature</u>. New York: Random, 1987.

Fey, Marion H. "Finding Voice through Computer Communication: A New Venue for Collaboration." <u>Journal of Advanced Composition</u> 14 (1994): 221-238.

Gerrard, Lisa, ed. <u>Writing at Century's End: Essays on Computer-Assisted Instruction</u>. New York: Random, 1987.

Greenleaf, Cynthia. "Technological Indeterminacy: The Role of Classroom Writing Practices and Pedagogy in Shaping Student Use of the Computer. <u>Written Communication</u> 11 (1994): 85-130.

Helpern, Jeanne M., and Sarah Ligget. <u>Computers and Composing</u>. Carbondale: Southern Illinois UP, 1984.

Handa, Carolyn, ed. <u>Computers and Community: Teaching Composition in the Twenty-First Century.</u> Boynton/ Cook.1990.

Hawisher, Gail E., "The Effects of Word Processing on the Revision Strategies of College Freshmen." <u>Research in the Teaching of English</u> 21 (1987): 145-59.

---, and Charles Moran. "Electronic Mail and the Writing Instructor." <u>College English</u> 55 (1993) 627-43.

---, and Cynthia L Selfe. <u>Critical Perspectives on Computers and Composition Instruction.</u> New York: Teachers College P of Columbia U, 1989.

---. <u>Evolving Perspectives on Computers and Composition Studies: Questions for the 1990s</u>. Urbana: NCTE, 1991.

---. "The Rhetoric of Technology and the Electronic Writing Class." <u>College Composition and Communication</u> 42 (1991): 55-65.

Hill, Charles A., David L. Wallace, and Christine Haas. "Revising On-Line: Computer Technologies and the Revising Process." <u>Computers and Composition</u> 1 (1990): 83-109.

Holdstein, Deborah. <u>On Composition and Computers</u>. New York: Modern Language Association, 1987.

---, and Cynthia L. Selfe. <u>Computers and Writing: Theory, Research, Practice</u>. New York: Modern Language Association, 1990.

Hult, Christine, and Jeanette Harris. <u>A Writer's Introduction to Word Processing</u>. Delmont, CA: Wadsworth, 1987.

Kline, Edward A. "Computers in the Humanities: Applications in Research and Instruction." <u>Computers and the Humanities</u>. Ed. C. Herbert Gilliland and Marlene Browne. Annapolis: U.S. Naval Academy. 1984. 1-23.

Klonoski, Edward. "Using the Eyes of the PC to Teach Revision." See **Revision.**

Koschman, T. D., ed. "Computer Support for Collaborative Learning." <u>Journal of the Learning Sciences</u> 3 (1993-94): 1-88.

Monroe, Rick. <u>Writing and Thinking with Computers: A Practical and Progressive Approach.</u> Urbana: NCTE, 1993.

Montague, Marjorie. <u>Computers, Cognition, and Writing Instruction.</u> Albany: State U of New York P. 1993.

Montroy, Trevor. "Speculation from A Practitioner in the Computer-Assisted Composition Classroom." <u>The Computer-Assisted Composition Journal</u> 9 (1994): 1-3.

Moran, Charles. "Computers and English: What Do We Make of Each Other?" Rev. of <u>Computers and Community</u>, by Carolyn Handa, ed.; <u>Computers and Writing: Theory, Research, Practice</u>, by Deborah H. Holstein and Cynthia L. Selfe, eds.; <u>Mindweave</u>, by Robin Masin and Anthony Kaye, eds. <u>College English</u> 54 (1992): 193-98.

Myers, Linda. <u>Approaches to Computer Writing Classrooms: Leaning for Practical Experience.</u> Albany: State U of New York P, 1994.

O'Brien, Sheila Ruzycki. "The Medium Facilitates the Message: Electronic Discourse and Literature Class Dynamics." See **Composition and Literature.**

Richard, Jack C., ed. <u>Error Analysis: Perspectives on Second Language Acquisition.</u> London: Longman, 1977.

Sadler, Lynn Veach. "The Computer-and-Effective Writing Movement: Computer-Assisted Instruction." <u>Association of Departments of English Bulletin</u> 87 (1987): 28-33.

Schwartz, Helen J. "Computer Perspectives: Mapping New Territories." Rev. of <u>Hypermedia and Literary Studies</u>, by Paul Delaney and George P. Landow, eds.; <u>Critical Perspectives on Computers and Composition Instruction</u>, by Gail E. Hawisher and Cynthia L. Selfe, eds.; <u>Evolving Perspectives on Computers and Composition Studies: Questions for the 1990's</u>, by Gail E. Hawisher and Cynthia L. Selfe, eds. <u>College English</u> 54 (1992): 207-12.

---. "Monsters and Mentors: Computer Applications for Humanistic Education." <u>College English</u> 44 (1982): 141-52.

---, Christine Y. Fitzpatrick, and Brian A. Huot. "The Computer Medium in Writing for Discovery." <u>Computers and Composition</u> 11 (1994): 137-49.

---, and Lillian S. Bridwell-Bowles. "A Selected Bibliography on Computers in Composition: An Update." <u>College Composition and Communication</u> 38 (1987): 453-57.

Selfe, Cynthia. <u>Creating a Computer-Supported Writing Facility: A Blueprint for Action.</u> Urbana: NCTE, 1989.

---, and Richard J. Selfe, Jr. "The Politics of Interface: Power and its Exercise in Electronic Contact Zones." <u>College Composition and Communication</u> 45 (1994): 480-504.

---, and Susan Hilligoss, eds. <u>Literacy and Computers: The Complications of Teaching and Learning with Technology.</u> New York: Modern Language Association, 1994.

Smith, John B. <u>Collective Intelligence in Computer-Based Collaboration.</u> See **Collaborative Writing.**

Sudol, Ronald A. "The Accumulative Rhetoric of Word Processing." <u>College English</u> 8 (1991): 920-32.

Sundermeier, Michael, and Bob Whipple. "Beginning the Computer Community: Establishing a Computerized Classroom." <u>The Computer-Assisted Composition Journal</u> 8 (1994): 41-47.

Susser, Bernard. "Word Processing and the Writing Process: A Review of Research." <u>The Computer-Assisted Composition Journal</u> 8 (1994): 28-37.

Takayoshi, Pamela. "Building New Networks from the Old: Women's Experiences With Electronic Communications." See **Composition and Gender.**

Taylor, Todd, and Joseph M. Moxley. "On Reviewing Electronic Discussions in Composition Studies." The Computer-Assisted Composition Journal 9 (1995): 18-21.

vander Geest, Thea, and Tim Remmers. "The Computer as Means of Communication for Peer-Review Groups." Computers and Composition 11 (1994): 237-250.

Vockell, Edward L., and Eileen Schwartz. "Microcomputers to Teach English Composition." Collegiate Microcomputer 6 (1988): 148-54.

Wresch, William, ed. The Computer in Composition Instruction, A Writer's Tool. Urbana: NCTE, 1984.

---, ed. The English Classroom in the Computer Age, Thirty Lesson Plans. Urbana; NCTE, 1991.

PLAGIARISM

Brown, Dorothy S. "The Perils of Plagiarism" College Composition and Communication 26 (1975): 206-207.

D'Angelo, Frank J. "The Art of Paraphrase." College Composition and Communication 30 (1979): 255-59.

Drum, Alice. "Responding to Plagiarism." College Composition and Communication 37 (1986): 241-43.

Friend, Christy. "Ethics in the Writing Classroom: A Nondistributive Approach." College English 56 (1994): 548-67.

Hatch, Gary L. The Crime of Plagiarism: A Critique of Literary Property Law. 1992. ERIC Ed 346-477.

Howard, Rebecca Moore. "Plagiarism and the Postmodern Professor." Journal of Teaching Writing 11 (1992): 233-45.

Kibler, William L., and Pamela Vannoy Kibler. "When Students Resort to Cheating." The Chronicle of Higher Education July 14, 1993 B1-2.

Kolich, Augustus M. "Plagiarism: The Worm of Reason." College English 45 (1983): 141-48.

Kroll, Barry M. "How College Freshman View Plagiarism." Written Communication 5 (1988): 203-21.

Martin, R. G. "Plagiarism and Originality: Some Remedies." English Journal 60 (1971): 621-28.

McCormick, Frank. "The Plagario and the Professor in Our Peculiar Institution." Journal of Teaching Writing 8 (1989): 133-46.

McLeod, Susan. "Responding to Plagiarism: The Role of the WPA." Writing Program Administration 15 (1992) 7-16.

Murphy, Richard. "Anorexa: The Cheating Disorder." College English 52 (1990): 898-903.

Roen, Duane H., and Geraldine McNenny. Collaboration as Plagiarism--Cheating Is in the Eye of the Beholder. 1992. ERIC ED 347-548.

Saalback, Robert Palmer. "Critical Thinking and the Problem of Plagiarism." College Composition and Communication 21 (1970): 45-47.

Sherrard, Carol. "Summary Writing: A Topological Study." Written Communication 3 (1986): 324-43.

Wells, Dorothy. "An Account of the Complex Causes of Unintentional Plagiarism in College Writing." Writing Program Administration 16 (1993): 59-71.

Whitaker, Elaine E. "A Pedagogy to Address Plagiarism." College Composition and Communication 44 (1993): 509-14.

PORTFOLIOS

Belanoff, Pat, and Marcia Dickson, eds. Portfolios: Process and Product. Portsmouth: Boynton/Cook, 1991.

---, and Peter Elbow. "Using Portfolios to Increase Collaboration and Community in a Writing Program." Journal of Writing Program Administration 9 (1986): 27-39.

Black, Laurel, et al., eds. New Directions in Portfolio Assessment: Reflective Practice, Critical Theory, and Large-Scale Scoring. Portsmouth. H: Boynton/Cook, 1995.

Bullock, Richard. "Spreading the Word . . . And Possibly Regretting It: Current Writing About Portfolios." Journal of Teaching Writing 12 (1995): 105-13.

Clark, Irene L. "Portfolio Evaluation, Collaboration, and Writing Centers." College Composition and Communication 44 (1993): 515-524.

Daiker, Don. New Directions in Portfolio Assessment. Ed. by Laurel Black et al. Portsmouth: Heinemann/Boynton-Cook, 1994.

Decker, Emily, George Cooper, and Susan Marie Harrington. "Crossing Institutional Boundaries: Developing an Entrance Portfolio to Improve Writing Instruction." Journal of Teaching Writing 12 (1992): 83-104.

Despain, LeRene, and Thomas L. Hilgers. "Readers' Responses to the Ration of Non-Uniform Portfolios: Are There Limits on Portfolios' Utility?" Writing Program Administration 16 (1992): 24-37.

Gill, Kent, ed. Process and Portfolios in Writing Instruction. Urbana: NCTE, 1993.

Hamp-Lyons, Liz, and William Condon. "Questioning Assumptions About Portfolio-Based Assessment." College Composition and Communication 44 (1993): 176-190.

Haswell, Richard, Lisa Johnson-Schull, and Susan Wyche-Smith. "Shooting Niagra: Making Portfolio Assessment Serve Instruction at a State University." Writing Program Administration 18 (1994): 44-55.

Herzig, Carl. "Portfolio Assessment as Faculty Development: The Small-School Context." Journal of Teaching Writing 12 (1992): 25-31.

Hesse, Douglas. "Portfolios and Public Discourse: Beyond the Academic/Personal Writing Polarity." Journal of Teaching Writing 12 (192): 1-12.

Hewitt, Geof. A Portfolio Primer: Teaching, Collecting, and Assessing Student Writing. Portsmouth, NH: Heinemann, 1995.

Kearns, Edward A. "On the Running Board of the Portfolio Bandwagon." Writing Program Administration 16 (1993): 50-58.

Kennedy, Mary Lyunch. "Using Portfolios to Assess a Composition Program." Composition Chronicle 5 (1992): 4-6.

McCleary, Bill. "NAEP Portfolio Study Gives Look at 'Real Writing' of U.S. Students." Composition Chronicle 8 (1995): 1-6.

Metzger, Elizabeth, and Lizbeth Bryant. "Portfolio Assessment: Pedagogy, Power, and the Student." Teaching English in the Two Year College 20 (1993): 279-88.

Porete, Carol, and Janell Cleland. The Portfolio as Learning Strategy. Portsmouth, NH: Boynton/Cook, 1994.

Porter, Carol, and Janell Cleland. The Portfolio as a Learning Strategy. Portsmouth, NH: Boynton/Cook, 1995.

Portfolio Assessment: An Annotated Bibliography of Selected Resources. Comp. Betty Hayes and Karen Johnson-Kretschman. Madison, WI: Madison Area Technical College, 1993.

Purves, Alan C., Joseph A. Quattrini, and Christine I. Sullivan. Creating the Writing Portfolio. Lincolnwood, IL: NTC Publishing, 1995.

Sommers, Jeffrey, Laurel Black, Donald A. Daiker, and Gail Stygall. "The Challenges of Rating Portfolios: What WPAs Can Expect." Writing Program Administration 17 (1993): 7-29.

Tierney, Robert J., Mark A. Carter, and Laura E. Desai. <u>Portfolio Assessment in the Reading-Writing Classroom</u>. Norwood, MA: Christopher-Gordon, 1991.

Yancy, Kathleen Blake, ed. <u>Portfolios in the Writing Classroom: An Introduction</u>. Urbana: NCTE, 1992.

PREWRITING AND INVENTION

Corbett, Edward P. J. <u>Classical Rhetoric for the Modern Student</u>. New York: Oxford UP, 1965. 94-174.

Elbow, Peter. <u>Writing with Power: Techniques for Mastering the Writing Process</u>. New York: Oxford UP, 1981.

Fulwiler, Toby. <u>The Journal Book</u>. Portsmouth, NH: Boynton/Cook, 1987.

Hillocks, George, Jr. <u>Research on Written Composition</u>. Urbana: ERIC, 1986. 169-86.

Huff, Roland, and Charles R. Kline, Jr. <u>A Contemporary Writing Curriculum: Composing and Valuing</u>. New York: Columbia UP, 1987. 1-51.

Murray, Donald M. "Write Before Writing." <u>College Composition and Communication</u> 29 (1978): 375-81.

Podis, JoAnne M., and Leonard M. Podus. "Identifying and Teaching Rhetorical Plans for Arrangement." <u>College Composition and Communication</u> 41 (1990): 430-42.

Proett, Jackie, and Kent Gill. <u>The Writing Process in Action: A Handbook for Teachers</u>. Urbana; NCTE, 1986.

Reynolds, Mark. "Make Free Writing More Productive." <u>College Composition and Communication</u> 39 (1988): 81-82.

Rohman, D. Gordon. "Pre-Writing: The Stage of Discovery in the Writing Process." <u>College Composition and Communication</u> 16 (1965): 106-12.

Rose, Mike. "Rigid Rules, Inflexible Plans, and the Stifling of Language." <u>College Composition and Communication</u> 31 (1980): 389-401.

---. <u>Writer's Block: The Cognitive Dimension</u>. Carbondale: Southern Illinois UP, 1984.

Swartzlander Susan, Deanna Pace, and Virginia Lee Stamler. "The Ethics of Requiring Students to Write about Their Personal Lives." <u>The Chronicle of Higher Education</u> Feb. 17, 1993, Section 2 B1-B2.

Tobin, Lad, and Thomas Newkirk, eds. <u>Taking Stock: The Writing Process Movement in the 90s</u>. Portsmouth, NH: Boynton/Cook, 1994.

Wallace, Karl L. "<u>Topoi</u> and the Problem of Invention." <u>Contemporary Rhetoric: A Conceptual Background with Readings</u>. Ed. W. Ross Winterowd. New York: Harcourt, 1975.

Wyche-Smith, Susan. "Teaching Invention to Basic Writers." <u>A Sourcebook for Basic Writing Teachers</u>. Ed. Theresa Enos. New York: Random, 1987. 470-79.

Young, Richard. "Recent Developments in Rhetorical Invention." <u>Teaching Composition: Twelve Bibliographic Essays</u>. Ed. Gary Tate. Fort Worth: Texas Christian UP, 1987. 1-38.

REVISION

Bamburg, Betty. "What Makes a Text Coherent?: <u>College Composition and Communication</u> 34 (1983): 417-29.

Brown, I., and T. E. Pearsall. <u>Better Spelling: Fourteen Steps to Spelling Improvement</u>. Lexington, MA: Heath, 1985.

Butturf, Douglas R., and Nancy L. Sommers. "Placing Revision in a Reinvented Rhetorical Tradition." <u>Reinventing the Rhetorical Tradition</u>. Eds. Avia Freedman and Ian Pringle. Conway: L & S Books, 1980. 99-104.

Beach, Richard. "Self-Evaluation Strategies of Extensive Revisers and Non-Revisers." <u>College Composition and Communication</u> 27 (1976): 160-64.

Berthoff, Ann E. "Recognition, Representation, and Revision." <u>Journal of Basic Writing</u> 3 (1981): 19-32.

Coe, Richard M. "If Not to Narrow, Then How to Focus: Two Techniques for Focusing." <u>College Composition and Communication</u> 32 (1981) 272-77.

D'Angelo, Frank. "The Topic Sentence Revisited." <u>College Composition and Communciation</u> 37 (1986): 431-41.

Faigley, Lester, and Stephen Witte. "Analyzing Revision." <u>College Composition and Communication</u> 32 (1981): 400-14.

Flower, Linda, et al. "Detection, Diagnosis, and the Strategies of Revision.""<u>College Composition and Communication</u> 37 (1986): 16-55.

---, and John R. Hayes. "Problem-Solving Strategies and the Writing Process." <u>College English</u> 39 (1977): 442-48.

Garrison, Roger, "One-to-One: Tutorial Instruction in Freshman Composition." <u>New Directions for Community Colleges</u> 2 (1974): 55-84.

Harris, Jeanette. "Proofreading: A Reading/Writing Skill." <u>College Composition and Communication</u> 38 (1987): 464-65.

Hartwell, Patrick. "Grammar, Grammars, and the Teaching of Grammar." <u>College English</u> 47 (1985): 105-27.

Klonoski, Edward. "Using the Eyes of the PC to Teach Revision." <u>Computers and Composition</u> 11 (1994): 71-78.

Krest, Margie. "Monitoring Student Writing: How Not to Avoid the Draft." <u>Journal of Teaching Writing</u> 7 (1988): 27-39.

Larson, Richard. "Sentences in Action: A Technique for Analyzing Paragraphs." <u>College Composition and Communication</u> 8 (1967): 16-22.

Markels, Robin B. <u>A New Perspective on Cohesion in Expository Paragraphs</u>. Carbondale: Southern Illinois UP, 1984.

Schwartz, Mimi. "Revision Profiles: Patterns and Implications." <u>College English</u> 45 (1983): 549-58.

Sommers, Nancy. "Revision Strategies of Student Writers and Experienced Adult Writers." <u>College Composition and Communication</u> 31 (1980): 378-88.

Sudol, Ronald, ed. <u>Revising: New Essays for Teachers of Writing</u>. Urbana: NCTE, 1982.

Witte, Stephen. "Topical Structure and Revision: An Exploratory Study." <u>College Composition and Communication</u> 34 (1983): 313-41.

SENTENCE COMBINING

Crowhurst, Marion. "Sentence Combining: Maintaining Realistic Expectations." <u>College Composition and Communication</u> 34 (1983): 62-72.

Daiker, Donald, Andrew Kerek, and Max Morenberg, eds. <u>Sentence Combining and the Teaching of Writing</u>. Conway, AK: L & S Books, 1979.

---, et al. <u>Sentence Combining: A Rhetorical Perspective</u>. Carbondale: Southern Illinois UP, 1985.

O'Hare, Frank. <u>Sentence Combining: Improving Student Writing Without Formal Grammar Instruction</u>. Urbana: NCTE, 1973.

---. <u>Sentencecraft: A Course in Sentence-Combining</u>. Lexington, MA: Ginn, 1985.

Strong, William. "Creative Approaches to Sentence Combining." 1986. ERIC ED 274 985.

---. <u>Sentence Combining: A Composing Book</u>. New York: Random, 1973.

---. <u>Sentence-Combining and Paragraph Building</u>. New York: Random, 1981.

STYLE

Addison, Catherine. "From Literal to Figurative: An Introduction to the Study of Simile." College English 55 (1993): 402-19.

Bernhardt, Stephen. "Seeing the Text." College Composition and Communication 37 (1986): 66-78.

Corbett, Edward P. J. "Approaches to the Study of Style." Teaching Composition: Twelve Bibliographic Essays. Ed. Gary Tate. Fort Worth: Texas Christian U, 1987.

Faigley, Lester. "Names in Search of a Concept: Maturity, Fluency, Complexity, and Growth in Written Syntax." College Composition and Communication 31 (1980): 219-300.

Graves, Richard. "A Primer for Teaching Style." College Composition and Communication 25 (1974): 186-90.

Hashimoto, I. "'Sentence Variety': Where Theory and Practice Meet and Lose." Composition Studies 21 (1993): 66-77.

Lanham, Richard. Analyzing Prose. New York: Scribner's, 1983.

Milic, Louis T. "Theories of Style and Their Implications for the Teaching of Composition." College Composition and Communication 16 (1965): 66-69, 126.

Miller, Edmund. Exercises in Style. Normal: Illinois State UP, 1980.

Selzer, Jack. "Exploring Options in Composing." College Composition and Communication 35 (1984): 276-84.

Walpole, Jane R. "The Vigorous Pursuit of Grace and Style." Writing Instructor 1 (1982): 163-69.

Weathers, Winston. An Alternate Style: Options in Composition. Rochelle Park, NJ: Hayden, 1980.

Williams, Joseph. Style: Ten Lessons in Clarity and Grace. 3rd ed. Glenview: Scott, 1989.

Winterowd, W. Ross. Composition/Rhetoric: A Synthesis. Carbondale: Southern Illinois UP, 1986. 55-65.

TEACHING COMPOSITION

Adams, Katherine H., and John L. Adams, eds. Teaching Advanced Composition: How and Why. Portsmouth: NH: Boynton, 1991.

Anson, Chris M., ed. Writing and Response: Theory, Practice, and Research. Urbana: NCTE, 1989.

Brand, Alice G., and Richard L. Graves, eds. Presence of Mind: Writing and the Domain Beyond the Cognitive. Portsmouth, NH: Heinemann Boynton/Cook, 1994.

Bridges, Charles W., ed. Training the New Teacher of College Composition. Urbana: NCTE, 1986.

Bullock, Richard H., and John Trembar. The Politics of Writing Instruction. Vol. 2. Portsmouth, NH: Heinemann, Boynton, 1990.

Caywood, Cynthia L., and Gillian R. Overing, eds. Teaching Writing: Pedagogy, Gender, and Equity. Albany: State U of New York P, 1987.

Coles, William E. Jr. The Plural I: The Teaching of Writing. New York: Holt, 1978.

Donovan, Timothy R., and Ben W. McClelland, eds. Eight Approaches to Teaching Composition. Urbana: NCTE, 1980.

Elbow, Peter. Embracing Contraries: Explorations in Learning and Teaching. New York: Oxford UP, 1986.

---. "Embracing Contraries in the Teaching Process." College English 45 (1983): 327-39.

Enos, Theresa, ed. A Sourcebook for Basic Writing Teachers. New York: Random, 1987.

Fitts, Karen, and Alan W. France, eds. Left Margins, Cultural Studies, and Composition Pedagogy. Albany: State U of New York P, 1995.

Foster, David A. A Primer for Writing Teachers: Theories, Theorists, Issues, Problems. 2nd ed. Upper Montclair, NJ: Boynton, 1992.

Garrison, Roger. One-to-One: Tutorial Instruction in Freshman Composition. Urbana: NCTE, 1986.

Graser, Elsa R. Teaching Writing: A Process Approach. Dubuque: Kendall/Hunt, 1983.

Graves, Richard L., ed. Rhetoric and Composition: A New Sourcebook for Teachers and Writers. 3rd ed. Upper Montclair: Heinemann, Boynton/Cook, 1990.

Hammond, Eugene R. Teaching Writing. New York: McGraw, 1983.

Harkin, Patricia, and John Schilb, eds. Contending with Words: Composition and Rhetoric in a Postmodern Age. New York: Modern Language Association, 1991.

Harris, Muriel. Teaching One-to-One: The Writing Conference. Urbana: NCTE, 1986.

Hillocks, George, Jr. Research on Written Composition: New Directions for Teaching. Urbana: NCRE-ERIC, 1986.

---. Teaching Writing as Reflective Practice. New York: Teachers College P, 1995.

Hult, Christine, ed. Evaluating Teachers of Writing. Urbana: NCTE, 1994.

Kline, Nancy. How Teachers Teach Writing. Englewood Cliffs, NJ: Prentice, 1992.

Knoblauch, C. H., and Lil Brannon. Rhetorical Traditions and the Teaching of Writing. Upper Montclair: Boynton/Cook, 1984.

Lindemann, Ericka. A Rhetoric for Writing Teachers. 2nd ed. New York: Oxford UP, 1987.

MacKenzie, Nancy. "Teaching the Composting Process: A Three-Part Project." The Writing Instructor 1 (1982): 103-11.

McCormick, Kathleen. The Culture of Reading and the Teaching of English. Manchester and New York: St. Martin's/Manchester UP, 1994.

Montroy, Trevor. "Computer-Assisted Composition Instruction: The Confessions of a Teacher About to Convert." The Computer-Assisted Composition Journal 8 (194): 26-27.

Myers, Miles, and James Gary, eds. Theory and Practice in the Teaching of Composition: Processing, Distancing, and Modeling. Urbana: NCTE, 1983.

Newkirk, Thomas, ed. Nuts and Bolts, A Practical Guide to Teaching College Composition. Portsmouth, NH: Boynton/Cook, 1993.

Patraglia-Bahri, Joseph, ed. Reconceiving Writing, Rethinking Writing Instruction. Hillsdale, NJ: Lawrence Erlbaum, 1995.

Peterson, Rae. The Writing Teacher's Companion: Planning Teaching and Evaluating in the Composition Classroom. Boston: Houghton Mifflin, 1995.

Quigley, Dan. "The Evolution on an On-line Syllabus." Computers and Composition 11 (1994) 165-71.

Randin, Elizabeth. Seeing Yourself As a Teacher: Conversations With Five New Teachers in a University Writing Program. Urbana: NCTE, 1994.

Rassmussen, Terry. Antifoundationalism: Can Believers Teach?" Rhetoric Review 13 (1994): 150-63.

Smagorinsky, Peter, and Melissa E. Whiting. How English Teachers Get Taught. Urbana: NCTE, 1995.

Smith, Maggie. Teaching College Writing. Boston: Allyn and Bacon, 1995.

Stang, Sonda J., and Robert Wiltenburg. Collective Wisdom: A Sourcebook of Lessons for Writing Teachers. New York: Random, 1988.

Sommer, Robert F. Teaching Writing to Adults: Strategies and Concepts for Improving Learner Performance. San Francisco: Jossey-Bass, 1989.

Spellmeyer, Kirt. Common Ground: Dialogue, Understanding, and the Teaching of Composition. Englewood Cliffs, NJ: Prentice Hall, 1993.

Tate, Gary, ed. <u>Teaching Composition: Twelve Bibliographic Essays</u>. Fort Worth: Texas Christian UP, 1994.

---, and Edward P. J. Corbett, and Nancy Myers, eds. <u>The Writing Teacher's Sourcebook</u>. 3rd ed. New York: Oxford UP, 1988.

Tompkins, Jane. "Pedagogy of the Distressed." <u>College English</u> 52 (1990): 653-60.

White, Edward M. <u>Assigning, Responding, Evaluating: A Writing Teacher's Guide (Including Diagnostic Tests)</u>. 2nd ed. New York: St. Martin's, 1992.

---. <u>Teaching and Assessing Writing</u>. 2nd ed. See **Assessment-Evaluation of Student Writing**

Williams, James D. <u>Preparing to Teach Writing</u>. Belmont: Wadsworth, 1989.

TEACHING ENGLISH AS A SECOND LANGUAGE

Allen, Harold B., ed. <u>Teaching English as a Second Language: A Book of Readings</u>. New York: McGraw-Hill, 1965.

Ashworth, Mary. <u>The First Step on the Longer Path: Becoming an ESL Teacher</u>. Portsmouth, NH: Heinermann, 1992.

Baker, Ann. <u>English to Get On With: Practice in Phrasal/Prepositional Verbs</u>. London: Heimemann, 1978.

Bander, Robert G. <u>American English Rhetoric: A Writing Program in English as a Second Language</u>. 2nd ed. New York: Holt, 1978.

<u>The Best Test Preparation for the TOEFL (Test of English as a Second Language)</u>. Piscataway, NJ: Research and Education Association, 1991.

Croft, Kenneth. <u>Readings on English as a Second Language for Teacher and Teacher Trainees</u>. 2nd ed. Cambridge: Winthrop, 1980.

Celce-Murcia, Marianne, and Diane Larsen-Freeman. <u>The Grammar Book: An ESL/EFL Teacher's Course</u>. Cambridge: Newbury House, 1983.

Chappel, Virginia A., and Judith Rodby. <u>Verb Tense and ESL Composition: A Discourse Level Approach</u>. 1982. ERIC ED 219 964.

Dean, Terry. "Multicutural Classrooms, Monocultural Teachers." <u>College Composition and Communication</u> 40 (1989): 23-37.

Frey, Betty J. <u>Basic Helps for Teaching English as a Second Language</u>. Tuscon: Polo Verde Publishing, 1970.

Goldman, Lorraine. <u>Getting Along with Idioms: Basic English Expressions and Two-word Verbs</u>. New York: Minerva Books, 1981.

Horning, Alice S. <u>Teaching Writing as a Second Language</u>. Carbondale: S. Illinois UP, 1987.

Harmer, Jeremy. <u>The Practice of English Language Teaching</u>. New York: Longman, 1983.

Johnson, Judith Anne. <u>Writing Strategies for ESL Students</u>. New York: Macmillan, 1983.

Kaplan, Robert B. "Contrastive Rhetoric and the Teaching of Composition." <u>Teachers of English to Speakers of Other Languages Quarterly</u> 1 (1967): 10-16.

Kroll, Barbara, ed. <u>Second Language Writing: Research Insights for the Classroom</u>. Cambridge: Cambridge UP, 1990.

Leki, Ilona. <u>Understanding ESL Writers: A Guide for Teachers</u>. Portsmouth, NH: Boynton-Cook, 1992.

Marcwardt, Albert H. <u>The Place of Literature in the Teaching of English as a Second on Foreign Language</u>. Honolulu: U of Hawaii P, 1978.

Master, Peter. "Teaching the English Article as a Binary System." <u>TESOL Quarterly</u> 24 (1990) 461-78.

Nelson, Gayle L., and John M. Murphy. "Peer Response Groups: Do L2 Writers Use Peer Comments in Revising Their Drafts?" <u>TESOL Quarterly</u> 27 (1993): 135-41.

Peyton, Joy Kreeft, and Jana Staton, eds. <u>Writing Our Lives: Reflections on Dialogue Journal Writing with Adults Learning English</u>. Englewood Cliffs, NJ: Prentice, 1991.

Reinhart, Susan M. <u>Testing Your Grammar</u>. Ann Arbor: U of Michigan P, 1985.

Rigg, Pat, and Virginia G. Allen, eds. <u>When They Don't All Speak English: Integrating the ESL Student into the Regular Classroom.</u> Urbana: NCTE, 1989.

Rinnert, Carol, and Mark Hansen. <u>Teaching the English Article System</u>. 1986. ERIC ED 284 436.

Rivers, Wilga M., and Mary S. Temperley. <u>A Practical Guide to the Teaching of English as a Second or Foreign Language</u>. New York: Oxford UP, 1978.

Sage, Howard. <u>Incorporating Literature in ESL Instruction</u>. Englewood Cliffs, NJ: Prentice-Hall, 1987.

Scarcella, Robin. <u>Teaching Language Minority Students in the Multicultural Classroom</u>. Englewood Cliffs, NJ: Prentice, 1990.

Schlumberger, Ann, and Diane Clymer. "Tailoring Composition Classes to ESL Students' Needs." <u>Teaching English in the Two-Year College</u> 16 (1989): 121-28.

<u>Second Language Writing: Research Insights for the Classroom</u>. New York: Cambridge UP, 1990.

Swales, John M. <u>Genre Analysis: English in Academic and Research Settings</u>. Cambridge: Cambridge UP, 1990.

Swan, Michael, and Bernard Smith, eds. <u>Learner English: A Teacher's Guide to Interference and Other Problems</u>. Cambridge: Cambridge UP, 1987.

Wattenmaker, Beverly S. <u>A Guidebook for Teaching English as a Second Language</u>. Boston: Allyn and Bacon, 1980.

Weir, Cyril J. <u>Evaluation in ELT.</u> New York: Blackwell, 1994.

Williams, James D. "English as a Second Language and Non-standard English." <u>Preparing to Teach Writing</u>. Belmont, CA: Wadsworth, 1989. 131-76.

<u>Writing Our Lives: Reflections on Dialogue Journal Writing with Adults Learning English</u>. Englewood Cliffs, NJ: Prentice Hall, 1991.

Wyatt, David H. <u>Computers and ESL</u>. Orlando: Harcourt, 1985

Zamel, Vivian. "Recent Research on Writing Pedagogy." <u>TESOL Quarterly</u> 21 (1987) 697-715.

WRITING ACROSS THE CURRICULUM

Anderson, Worth, Cynthia Best, Alycia Black, John Hurst, Brandt Miller, and Susan Miller. "Cross-Curricular Underlife: A Collaborative Report on Ways with Academic Words." <u>College Composition and Communication</u> 41 (190): 11-36.

Andrews, Deborah C., and Margaret D. Blickle. <u>Technical Writing: Principles and Forms</u>. 2nd ed. New York: Macmillan, 1982.

Anson, Chris M., John E. Schwiebert, and Michael M. Williamson, comps. <u>Writing Across the Curriculum: An Annotated Bibliography</u>. Westport, CT: Greenwood, 1993.

Barnet, Sylvan. <u>A Short Guide to Writing About Art</u>. 4th ed. New York: HarperCollins, 1993.

Bizell, Patricia, and Bruce Herzberg. "Writing Across the Curriculum: A Bibliographic Essay." <u>The Territory of Language: Linguistics, Stylistics, and the Teaching of Composition</u>. Ed. Donald A. McQuade. 2nd ed. Carbondale: Southern Illinois UP, 1986.

Blair, Catherine Pastore. "Only One of the Voices: Dialogic Writing Across the Curriculum." <u>College English</u> 50 (1988): 383-89.

Bowles-Bridwell, Lillian. "Freedom, Form, Function: Varieties of Academic Discourse." College Composition and Communication 46 (1995): 46-61.

Brunner, Ingrid, et al. The Technician as Writer: Preparing Technical Reports. Indianapolis: Bobbs, 1980.

Brusaw, Charles T., et al. The Business Writer's Handbook. 3rd ed. New York: St. Martin's, 1987.

Carson, Jay. "Recognizing and Using Context as a Survival Tool for WAC." Writing Program Administration 17 (1994): 35-47.

Cuba, Lee. A Short Guide to Writing about Social Science. 2nd ed. NY: HarperCollins, 1993.

Dick, John A. R., and Robert M. Esch. "Dialogues Across Disciplines: A Plan for Faculty Discussions of Writing Across the Curriculum." College Composition and Communication 36 (1985): 178-82.

Fulwiler, Toby. "How Well Does Writing Across the Curriculum Work?" College English 46 (1984): 113-25.

---. "The Argument for Writing Across the Curriculum." Writing Across the Disciplines: Research into Practice. Ed. Art Young and Toby Fulwiler. Upper Montclair: Boynton/Cook, 1986.

---. "The Personal Connection: Journal Writing Across the Curriculum." Language Connections. Urbana: NCTE, 1982. 15-31.

---, and Arthur W. Biddle, gen. eds. A Community of Voices: Reading and Writing in the Disciplines. New York: Macmillan, 1992.

---, and Art Young, eds. Language Connections: Writing and Reading Across the Curriculum. Urbana: NCTE, 1982.

---, and Art Young, eds. Programs That Work: Models and Methods for Writing Across the Curriculum. Portsmouth, NH: Heinemann, Boynton/Cook, 1990.

Galindo, Rene, and Constance Brown. "Person, Place, and Narrative in an Amish Farmer's Appropriation of Nature Writing." Written Communication 12 (1995): 147-185.

Gregg. L., and E. Steinberg, eds. Cognitive Processes in Writing: An Interdisciplinary Approach. Hillsdale, NJ: Urlbaum, 1980.

Griffin, C. Williams, ed. Teaching Writing in All Disciplines. San Francisco: Jossey-Bass, 1982.

Herrington, Anne, and Charles Moran, eds. Writing, Teaching, and Learning in the Disciplines. New York: Modern Language Association, 1992.

Howard, Rebecca M., and Sandra Jamieson. The Bedford Guide to Teaching Writing in the Disciplines: An Instructor's Desk Reference. New York: Bedford Books of St. Martin's P, 1995.

Kinneavy, James L. "Writing Across the Curriculum." Association of Departments of English Bulletin 76 (1983): 14-21.

Kirscht, Judy, Rhonda Levine, and John Reiff. "Evolving Paradigms: WAC and the Rhetoric of Inquiry." College Composition and Communication 45 (1994): 369-80.

LaNano, Mari. "Computerized Collaboration in Technical Professional Composition." The Computer-Assisted Composition Journal 6 (1992): 30-32.

Larson, Richard L. "Writing in the Disciplines: Facilitating Invention." Composition Chronicle 5 (1992): 8-9.

Mahala, Daniel. "Writing Utopias: Writing Across the Curriculum and the Promise of Reform." College English 53 (1991): 773-89.

Maimon, Elaine P. "Maps and Genres: Exploring Connections in the Arts and Sciences." Composition and Literature: Bridging the Gap. Ed. Winifred Bryan Horner. Chicago: U of Chicago P, 1983.

Maimon, Elaine P. "Writing Across the Curriculum: Past, Present, and Future."
    <u>Teaching Writing in All Disciplines</u>. Ed. C. Williams Griffin. San Francisco:
    Jossey-Bass, 1982.
Maimon, Elaine P., et al. <u>Writing in the Arts and Sciences</u>. Cambridge: Winthrop, 1981.
Maruis, Richard. <u>A Short Guide to Writing About History</u>. 2nd ed. New York:
    HarperCollins, 1995.
Masiello, Lea. <u>Write at the Start: A Guide to Using Writing in Freshman Seminars</u>.
    Columbia, SC: National Resource Center for the Freshman Year Experience,
    1993.
McLeod, Susan H., ed. <u>Strengthening Programs for Writing Across the Curriculum</u>. San
    Francisco: Jossey-Bass, 1988.
Moffett, James. <u>Active Voice: A Writing Program Across the Curriculum</u>. Portsmouth;
    Boynton/Cook, 1981.
Picket, Nell Ann, and Ann A. Laster. <u>Technical English: Writing, Reading, and
    Speaking</u>. 4th ed. New York: Harper, 1984.
Porush, David. <u>A Short Guide to Writing about Science</u>. New York: HarperCollins,
    1995.
Russel, David R. "Writing Across the Curriculum in Historical Perspective: Toward a
    Social Interpretation." <u>College English</u> 52 (1990): 52-73.
Siegel, Muffy E. A., and Toby Olsen, eds. <u>Writing Talks: Views on Teaching Writing
    from Across the Professions</u>. Upper Montclair: Boynton/Cook, 1983.
Sensenbaugh, Roger. "Studies on Effectiveness of Writing-across-the-Curriculum
    Programs." <u>Composition Chronicle</u> 5 (1992): 8-9.
Schmidt, Diane E. <u>Expository Writing in Political Science: A Practical Guide</u>. New
    York: HarperCollins, 1993.
Smith, Louise Z. "Why English Departments Should 'House' Writing Across the
    Curriculum." <u>College English</u> 50 (1988): 390-95.
Stockton, Sharon. "Writing in History: Narrating the Subject of Time." <u>Written
    Communication</u> 12 (1995): 47-73.
Stratton, Charles R. <u>Technical Writing: Process and Product</u>. New York: Holt, 1984.
Tchudi, Sephen, ed. <u>The Astonishing Curriculum: Integrating Science and Humanities
    Through Language</u>. Urbana: NCTE, 1993.
Stuart, Ann. <u>The Technical Writer</u>. New York: Holt, 1988.
Thralls, Charlotte. <u>Technical Writing Theory and Practice</u>. New York: Modern
    Language Association, 1989.
Vande Kopple, William J. "Some Characteristics and Functions of Grammatical Subjects
    in Scientific Discourse." <u>Written Communication</u> 11 (1994): 534-64.
Walvoord, Barbara E. Fassler. <u>Helping Students Write Well: A Guide for Teachers in All
    Disciplines</u>. 2nd ed. New York: Modern Language Association, 1986.
Winsor, Dorothy A. "Invention and Writing in Technical Work." <u>Written
    Communication</u> 112 (1994): 227-50.

NOTES

NOTES

NOTES

NOTES

NOTES

NOTES

NOTES

NOTES

NOTES

NOTES

NOTES

NOTES